THE BOOK OF QUESTIONS AND ANSWERS

by
Joshua Coltrane

SANTA MONICA PRESS
P.O. Box 1076
Santa Monica, CA 90406-1076
Printed in the United States

TABLE OF CONTENTS

The Animal Kingdom

Why do cats' eyes appear to glow in the dark?

That eerie yellowish-green "eye shine" is produced by a part of the cat's eye called "tapetum lucidum." It's a layer behind the retina that acts like a mirror, allowing light to pass back out through the retina. This means a cat has two chances to see light, which is useful because it does most of its hunting at night (or used to, before we started feeding it Friskies). The shine tends to be more visible at night, because the cat's pupils are usually dilated to allow in more light.

What's the best way to relate dog and cat years to human years?

Dogs and cats both mature sexually at about nine months; dogs then live an average of between 12 and 14 years, cats 15 to 17 years. The best formula for dogs is to call the first year about 21, then add five years for each human year thereafter. Thus, a five-year-old dog is 21 + (4 X 5 = 20), or 41 years old in human terms. For cats, call the first year 15, then add seven from there on. So a five-year-old cat is 15 + (4 X 7 = 28), or 43 years old in human terms.

Do horses sleep standing up?

Most do, yes. Horses actually find it more comfortable to lock their knees in a standstill position, so they sleep that way. Their bodies are so heavy that when they lie down they have trouble breathing—it could even kill them. Most only lie down when they're sick or when a mare is foaling (giving birth).

Are cats colorblind?

No, they just don't care much about color. They're nocturnal, you see, so it's more important to them to detect the difference between black and white, as well as motion and stillness, for hunting purposes.

Scientists have tested and tested cats for this, and found that it took an extraordinary number of tries for them to learn the difference between, say, green and gray. They eventually got the hang of it, proving they could, and the scientists reasoned they were just very slow learners. But a later conclusion makes more sense: they just didn't care enough about it.

Which animals cannot reproduce?

Mules. They are the offspring of a male donkey and a female horse, which has proven to be an ideal combination over time. You get the horse's good looks and trainability as well as a donkey's resistance to disease and extreme willingness to work slavishly. What you don't get is a mule population, because all male and most female mules are born sterile. If you couldn't reproduce, you'd have nothing better to do than work all your life, too.

Why don't birds die of electrocution when they perch on wires?

Because they aren't grounded. In order to be electrocuted, you have to have a complete circuit, meaning one part of you has to touch a live current while another part of you touches a dead one. The electricity from the live side would then flow through you to get to the dead side. Meanwhile, you light up like a bulb. If you're a bird, you only touch one side—the electricity therefore doesn't bother you; it just continues on its merry way. So the more important question is, if you're a bird, how do you know all this?

How do birds know where to migrate?

In addition to their fine sense of electricity, birds are also amateur astronomers. They sense their direction based on their relative position to the stars. One scientist observed starlings in a planetarium, and noted that they always navigated their course by means of Polaris, the North Star. Even when he reversed Polaris' planetarium position so that it appeared due south, they still followed it.

Other bird experts believe they navigate based on a strong sense of magnetic fields, especially since they know better than to fly on rainy nights—it's that electrical expertise again.

Why do skunks make that awful stench?

It's their defense mechanism. All animals had to have at least one in order to evolve this far; some are just more unique than others. A porcupine's quills, for instance. Or an owl's ability to rotate his head, to see predators (and prey) from any direction. So the skunk has evolved this special ability to survive by defeating larger, faster enemies with his body oil, which is produced in his scent glands, then shot at distances of eight to ten feet at his attackers, causing temporary blindness and vomiting. It's so strong that even us humans, who did nothing to provoke him, smell it from the freeway.

Do elephants ever forget?

Apparently not. One German professor decided to find out for sure a few years ago. He marked two boxes, one with a square and one with a circle, and placed food in the box with the square. After 330 tries, Dumbo finally got the idea that "square" meant "food." (There's no I.Q. test for being King of Beasts.) But the remarkable thing is that the professor returned a year later with the same test—square and circle. The result? No problem. Dumbo went right for the square. This explains elephants' perennial status as circus regulars. It takes a while, but once they learn a trick, they remember it forever.

Is there a species in which males give birth?

Seahorses. Somehow, when Mother Nature was giving mating lessons, this breed got confused. Female seahorses initiate the dance by depositing eggs in the males' pouches, who then fertilize them with sperm, incubate them, and give birth to them, as many as 300 in 20 minutes. Weirder still, Pop then eats most of his young when he swims past them, not recognizing what they are.

Why do cats purr?

Because they're happy, of course. When they're kittens, they feel their mother vibrate when they feed, and identify the pleasure of feeding with the purr, thus learning to purr whenever they're similarly contented. They also, however, use it during fear or distress, although cat lovers will no doubt notice a strong difference in tone between the two.

Why are cats so afraid of water?

They're really not. Their cousins, tigers and jaguars, are always pouncing on alligators in rivers in the jungle. Your average house cats, though, are neat freaks, and they're also lazy. Felix Unger and Oscar Madison in the same little body, in a way. They have this thing about being well-groomed, which in their minds means a cat saliva shower. They figure if they get wet, they'll get that water stuff all over them, and have to start the self-licking process all over again. Unlike your dog Spot, who happily flops himself into the ocean just to retrieve a stick, then showers *you*, it's a different story for your cat Scarlett—for her, there's nothing interesting in there, she'll mess up her hair, and well, it's just not worth it.

What's the best way to make friends with a dog?

First, remove anything you may be carrying, such as a backpack, a television set, or a keg of beer, so that you appear in human form to the dog. Otherwise, Fido may perceive you as some weird mutant with a strange new form, and be on his guard.

Second, speak slowly and calmly to Fido. Do not raise your voice, as this tone is reserved only for reprimands ("*bad* dog, Fido") or emergencies ("Fido! Help!"). But Fido is not a genius, so speak in simple, even baby-ish tones. Animal expert Barbara Woodhouse believes the word "what" is a magical all-purpose word ("*what* a nice dog!").

Third, let the dog come to you. Even if he slobbers all over you, stand your ground. "Stay" is helpful in that instance. But don't extend your hand too far. That could be interpreted as a sign of fear. Instead, keep it fairly close to your body and open your palm. Fido will usually walk over, sniff it, give it a lick, and then you're all palsy-walsy.

Then, and only then, should you pet him. Many dogs resent being pawed until they've introduced themselves to you and given you the go-ahead. Once you're on solid terms, try petting him softly on his upper chest. This is sort of a secret, sensitive part of Fido's physiognomy, and touching it (once you're friends) is like sharing a secret between the two of you, and will surely enamor him of you.

Why do roosters crow in the morning?

For the same reason a dog barks at you when you walk by. They're declaring their territory. They're saying, "I own this joint, I own these hens, stay off my cotton-picking property." Barnyard fowl are most active in the wee hours of the morning—it's their social hour—so that's why they do their bellowing then. If they crow at other hours, it's usually for roll-call purposes: if other chickens are wandering too far from the flock, it's their job to let them know where home is.

Can chickens run around with their heads cut off?

This bit of animal lore was finally proven in 1945 in an issue of Life magazine, which ran a photo and story of one such unlucky fowl. Mike the chicken was chosen as dinner one day by a farmer named L.A. Olsen. Olsen missed, however, and only chopped off three-fourths of Mike's head, leaving his brain stem intact. Since this is the part of a chicken that actually operates the heart and lungs, Mike just kept on puttering around the barnyard. Olsen not only took photos, he fed Mike for several weeks with an eyedropper, and even stuffed corn down his throat. Presumably, Mike eventually became the evening meal, but look what a legacy he gave to the world of animal science.

How did the Chihuahua get its name?

Chihuahua, the northern state of Mexico, was the first place this smallest of dogs was discovered by those people who make notes of dog breeds in dog books. It had been there awhile, having descended from a Techichi, a tiny mute dog kept by the Mexican Toltec tribe since the ninth century A.D.

Did flea circuses really exist?

Yes, they just got out-marketed by those darn

rock concerts and football games! To begin with, there wasn't all that much money in it. The circus owner could only fit about six or seven seats around the circus table, so he staged as many shows as he could in an hour.

A few flea tricks: pull each other in tiny wagons; playing wee instruments in a flea orchestra; dancing, card playing, acrobatics . . . you name it. Most of the top flea stars died out, though. Today it's even harder to find that special superstar flea talent, mostly for nutritional reasons. In the old, dirtier days, you see, fleas survived quite a bit on the blood of humans. Now that we all use Dial each morning, most fleas have resorted to dog and cat plasma for their diet, which just isn't as peppy as ours.

How do flies walk on the ceiling?

Very carefully. Actually, flies are blessed with special anatomical gifts for just this purpose. To us, a ceiling is flat. But in their microscopic world, the ceiling is full of ridges and valleys. Each of their six legs, therefore, has a pair of tiny claws for grasping and suction cup-like pads for sticking.

The bigger question is, how do they turn themselves upside down before they land? With a fly backflip, of course. Hey, fleas can turn acrobatic tricks, why can't flies?

Do animals have their own vocabularies?

Of course. Much has been made of the "languages" of whales and dolphins, but most other species "talk" to each other, too. Scientists have reported 17 different versions of "meow" for cats, each with its own meaning (if you own a cat, you've probably learned a few yourself). Most species have different sounds or inflections for food, danger, contentment, mating, and that sort of thing. A rooster crows to let the other chickens know he is in charge. Some male horses—those with the pack-leader instinct—whinny for the same reasons in the stables. Many pack animals, like wolves and birds, have distress and food calls. The list goes on, but you get the idea.

Is a crocodile the same as an alligator?

No. An alligator is actually a subspecies of a crocodile, and is different in several ways: his snout is more rounded (the croc's is pointy); his teeth don't show when he closes his mouth, unlike a croc; and he's not as aggressive as a croc, so if you decide to wrestle one or the other to impress your date, choose the 'gator.

What species is Goofy?

In the film *Stand By Me,* four boys discuss this strange phenomenon: no one seems to know what kind of animal Goofy is. He walks on two feet, speaks befuddled English, and bears no resemblance to other characters. So what is he?

He's a dog. An unusual dog, yes, but a dog. He looks nothing like Pluto, an obvious dog, because Pluto was drawn as Mickey's (originally Minnie's) pet, so to be subservient, Pluto walks on all fours and barks. Goofy, however, was created to be his own man, not a pet, therefore he's equal in the animation world to Mickey and the gang. But he's still a dog.

Do any fish sleep?

Some do. In coral reefs, some sleep standing up on their tails. Others lean on rocks. But most fish don't have eyelids (except for sharks and rays), so they can't very well close them and nod off to neverland. Besides, what if a bigger fish came along and ate them while they were snoozing? Nope, this just doesn't happen. Many fish *never* stop swimming (it's how they breathe, you know). The rest just tune out the boring stuff every now and then, kinda like how we never notice the same old road signs when we're driving to work.

Does a hummingbird actually hum?

A hummingbird flaps its wings so fast—about 40 to 50 times per second—that the resulting noise sounds like a hum to us. It also flies at speeds up to 700 miles per hour, so don't try to outrun it, especially if you're an insect. It'll corner you and suspend itself in the air like a helicopter, then eat you; or if you're a plant, suck your nectar. Sounds like living, huh?

What's the difference between a pig and a hog?

Here in America, we care about such things. We have a rule, to wit: all swine under 180 pounds are pigs; over 180, they're hogs. In England, they're all pigs. What do they know?

What is the origin of the Thoroughbred horse?

Humans have been racing horses since the Roman era, but each culture had its own breed: the English, for instance, raced fast Scottish ponies called Galloways; the Irish raced their own ponies, called "hobby horses." But soon competitiveness in the British Isles led to importing Italian and Spanish horses to win races. The stock thus became diluted.

Enter King Charles II of England, a betting man. Around 1660, he ordered "12 extraordinary good colts" from the Royal Stud master, who, embarrassed at the pickings, imported "pure" Arabians. For the next century, this "new" breed flourished, and three in particular stood out. Every racehorse, show jumper, and steeplechaser you see today is descended from these three fine Arabians.

Noted for their long, graceful stride and precocity—they race as early as two years old—Thoroughbreds have evolved into taller and faster horses, but they're also more nervous and fragile than most animals, due to centuries of inbreeding.

How do camels survive without water?

Well, they do need water, but they can go a long time between fill-ups. They can drink up to 25 gallons in one pit stop rather quickly, then travel across a blazing desert for days.

Contrary to popular belief, they don't store water in their humps. If they did, their backs would gradually flatten after a few days—have you ever seen a hump-less camel? Didn't think so. No, they deplete it from their body tissue. Most mammals lose it from their blood, which becomes increasingly thicker until it can't metabolize heat so well. So why don't *we* switch to the tissue method? Sure would help those folks in Arizona.

Why do flies circle around nothing so much?

It may be nothing to you, but to them it's a dream date, a dance of courtship, a tango of love—well, usually. Long fluorescent light bulbs are even more attractive than their mate.

Why are dogs loyal and cats aloof?

Back before they were both lazy house pets, dogs and cats used to have to work for their food. Hard to believe, yes.

Dogs are descended from wolves, and wolves are pack animals. Their system is basically follow-the-leader. So if you introduce yourself as master to a puppy before he's about eight weeks old, he will acknowledge you as, in a sense, "pack leader," and do whatever you wish. (After eight weeks, he's going to figure he's on his own, and will never oblige.) In his mind, he makes the following deal: *You bring in the food for the pack, and I'll follow your orders and circle the camp, er, yard, at night to protect it from invaders.* A blissful arrangement for all.

Cats, on the other hand, are solitary hunters in the wild. They fend for themselves using stealth and speed. We tamed them exactly for these qualities—to trap and eat all the annoying mice that would chew away at our food stores. But we dulled their hunting instincts over time by giving them Friskies every day. So now we're left with a creature who's a bit confused. He wants to hunt, but he doesn't need to. So he just chases little birds and swats at them. Drags a rat in the house every now and then to let us know we haven't bred out all of his talents yet. He's also learning to be more social, but it takes a lot of evolving for a species to become completely dopey, helpless, and lovable.

The Human Body

What actually happens when one of your limbs "falls asleep?"

Amputation. You know—you wake up in the middle of the night and suddenly, in a panic, you realize you're paralyzed. You can't move your arm—it just flops around. You think, "Oh, please no, I *need* this arm." After a few more flops, it gradually comes back to life, you are whole again, you sigh with relief, you fall back asleep.

Okay, so it's no big deal. It's called "neurapraxia," and all that happens is that in your strange sleeping position, you compressed a nerve between a bone and another hard object—say, the wall. The blood still circulates, thank heavens.

What is itching?

Amazingly, no one knows for sure. Doctors have given it a fancy-schmantzy name—"punctate puritus"—but that's all they've got. They know it's related to nerve-endings and the sense of pain, since people who stop feeling pain also stop itching (songwriters figure that if you can still feel the pain of a broken heart, you can still itch to love again), but the rest, well, they're working on it. Assuming, of course, you don't have fleas or poison oak, arbitrary spot itching—like the common cold—remains a great mystery.

Do we have any cells that don't regenerate?

Brain cells. If they're destroyed by injury, lack of oxygen, drug use, or thinking too hard (OK—not), they're gone forever. If you lose too many brain cells, deafness, blindness, loss of speech, or paralysis can result. Brain cells actually die every day from the day you're born—up to 100,000 a day around age 60. However, in spite of this, some scientists believe your I.Q. may increase with age.

How many times does a heart beat in an average life?

If we set a typical life span at 70 years, and a pulse rate of at least once per second (this is quite normal), it comes out to 2.8 billion heartbeats. One of the benefits of leading a healthy lifestyle with regular exercise, then, is a lowered resting pulse, which, if you do the math, translates to a longer life expectancy.

What is "tone deafness?"

Another excuse for laziness, essentially. It's one thing to have a legitimate hearing impairment, in which all sounds are difficult to understand. But all normal hearing persons can hear tones if they can hear anything else. If they can't carry a tune, they just never bothered to try.

Why do you wake up just before your alarm goes off?

You think it's because you made a mental note to yourself, right? On important days, say, your wedding, when you *have* to get up, you tell yourself, "I *have* to wake up at 7 A.M.," and lo and behold, your eyes are popping at 6:59, just before the clock radio begins blaring.

What gives? Well, it's two things. First, your circadian rhythms. These dictate, among other functions, the ebb and flow of your body temperature. At night, your body temperature usually drops to its lowest point around 4 A.M., then gradually rises until you wake up. In the last hour or two of sleep, you're not technically awake yet, but you're aware of things.

This means you're aware enough to hear the faint click that alarm clocks make just before they go off. You don't realize you hear it, *but you do.*

What are goose bumps?

A relic of a bygone era—specifically, our hairier days in caves. Back then, when it got very cold, our hair would stand on end, trapping air and insulating us. Nowadays, we have groovy leather jackets for that. But the skin still thinks it has hair, and bristles to get warm. Hey, don't knock it, it's just trying to help.

What is 20/20 vision?

Confusing. Here's why. First of all, the first number is always 20. It refers to what you can see at 20 feet, relative to a "normal" person. So if the second number is also a 20, it means you can read letters on a chart that a normal person can also read at 20 feet. You're cool. But if you have, say, 20/50 vision, it means you can only read at 20 feet what Joe Normal can read at 50. You're falling behind him. If you have 20/10, what you can read at 20 feet he has to stand 10 feet closer to see. You win. So you, er, see, it's that Joe fella that's always moving. How silly.

How much of our brains do we actually use?

Contrary to myth, we *do* use every part of it. Come on, why else would it be there? It's just that we don't use every part of it *at the same time*. Typically, we use about five percent at any moment, but usage from lobe to lobe jumps around depending on the activity—figuring your taxes is *here*, remembering cocktail party jokes is *there*, planning your next move in a chess game is *over there*—you get the idea.

Why do we have two nostrils?

You'd be surprised how clever your nose is. We have two nostrils so that when one is clogged, we can still breathe through the other one. You'll notice you never experience the clogging of both at once. This is because the nostrils *take turns* housing the offending phlegm.

How can this be, you ask? Well, each nostril is also controlled by each of our lungs. If one nostril were always clogged, that corresponding lung would be in danger. We unconsciously help this switching process along when we sleep. If one nostril is stuffed for awhile, we naturally roll over to our other side, moving the phlegm with it. Thus each lung survives. Miracles never cease.

If you sold your entire body, how much would you get for it?

Think about this for a second. Okay. Now, assuming there *was* still a you after you sold yourself, how rich would you be?

Not very rich, if you sold it all at once. The key is to market it intelligently—you know, buy ads in the scientific journals, maybe write some catchy copy, like, "tastes great . . . less fillings" or something.

Seriously, people have been known to run classifieds advertising certain organs—a kidney, say, for ten thousand dollars. Those waiting for a kidney transplant would presumably be interested, and, hey, the seller still has another one left over.

If you did this piece by piece, "you" would probably end up with about $175,000. Plenty for a Gucci wardrobe, if "you" had a body to wear it with.

What is the cause of a "brain freeze," or "ice cream headache?"

Believe it or not, the actual medical term for this phenomenon is, in fact, "ice cream headache." Somebody goofed. They were supposed to call it "Hypothermal Haagen-Daszia" or some such.

Once again, doctors are stumped. You'd think they'd pay attention to things that really matter—*that all of us get*—instead of researching a cure for, oh, lung cancer. Their best guess is that the coldness of the dessert constricts the blood vessels in the mouth region. Since blood has to flow *somewhere,* it rushes on up to the head, which overstretches those blood vessels there, resulting in pain. Suggestion: eat slower, warm up the goodies in the mouth, savor the taste *and* feel no pain.

How do hair and nails grow after death?

They don't. It's a myth. Growing requires nourishment from blood. No blood flow, no go. It's actually another illusion, caused by the body drying up. The skin contracts about a sixteenth of an inch, revealing a bit more of the hair and nails.

What causes yawns to be contagious?

Again, doctors are stumped (see: itching). What do we pay them for, anyway?

But, oh, how this is true. The mere word has already caused you to yawn, hasn't it? See, there you go again. Just try to resist it. If we could harness the power of yawn suggestion, we could control the world!!

Some people believe we yawn for lack of oxygen, or because the room's too warm. Then there's the nervous yawn. The awkward first-date conversation lull yawn. The faux-polite "gee, it's getting late" yawn.

Another of life's great mysteries.

What causes bad breath in the morning?

Bad breath is a sulfur smell, and it's created by hungry microorganisms feasting on leftovers. The result of their munching is a chemical reaction that ends up in a sulfur odor emanating from your 8 A.M. yawn. These playful bacteria enjoy the food between your teeth, the plaque on your teeth, the dead tissue your mouth is shedding, and the little pools of saliva that have been stagnant like a pond in your mouth all night.

How do you fight them off? You know all this. Brush and floss, of course. It not only lengthens the life of your teeth, it improves your breath, and thusly, your social life.

There's one other solution: you can stay up all night talking. A constant flow of saliva is actually the best way to wash away all this flotsam and jetsam—this is why bad breath is less likely during the day, when you're yapping, chewing, and swallowing a lot. So unless you're an avid sleeptalker—and we're talking *verbose*—you can look forward to a sulfuric sunrise.

After you eat, how long should you wait before going swimming?

Unless you've been living on Mars lately, you know this is a huge practical joke, originated by some fun-loving lifeguard or wacky water-safety instructor. People actually believed they'd get a stomach cramp and drown. How many news stories have you read of this actually happening? Boy Drowns From Stomach Cramps. Witnesses Say He Ate Lunch Twenty Minutes Earlier.

Bah. Cramps are rare, according to research. It's probably not wise to backstroke the English Channel on a full stomach, but if you suddenly decide to go cavorting in the pool or ocean, well, bonzai.

Household Mysteries

If bath towels only touch clean skin, why do they grow stiff and smelly after only a few days?

It's not you. It's your dead skin. Even though you've removed dirt and germs in the shower, there's still dead skin that sticks to the cotton towel as you dry.

The other problem is ventilation. Humid bathrooms are spawning grounds for mildew. To offset this, it's best to open a window after you shower, not so much *while* you shower. If you don't let it breathe, it'll soon smell like your junior high school locker room—ugh.

What, exactly, is glass?

Believe it or not, glass is a liquid. That's how you can see through it. If you examine a very old window, you'll notice that it's thicker and rounded on the bottom. That's because the glassy liquid has sunk over the years due to the pull of gravity.

Glass is transparent because its molecules are spaced loosely, like in other liquids, so as not to block out light. It's also designed not to absorb, reflect, or bend light, so it can better perform its see-through function.

How does a Thermos work? How does it know what to keep cold and what to keep hot?

It's a vacuum. There are actually two containers in a Thermos—a glass bottle inside of a metal outer container. In between is nothingness—zero air molecules, or as close to zero as the manufacturer could get.

In a vacuum, without going into scientific details, the temperature of a substance will remain the same, because heat will not pass in or out. So if your Thermos is holding coffee, it will keep the heat in. If it's holding cold milk, it will keep the heat from the outside from entering.

How does soap remove dirt?

There are two types of dirt: greasy and non-greasy. To remove non-greasy dirt, all you need is water. No problem. But water is useless on greasy dirt, for the same reason it won't put out a grease fire, because, as everyone knows, oil and water don't mix.

Soap is ideal because its molecules are two-sided. One side attracts grease like a magnet attracts aluminum shavings, while the other side attracts water. So, first the greasy dirt molecules are gobbled up by soap molecules, then the soap molecules are surrounded by water molecules, which are easily drained away. One of life's little miracles.

How does a phone cord get so twisted?

You think it's the phone company's idea of a cruel joke, don't you? They design these things so they'll automatically curl up over time, causing the line to crackle and, ultimately, causing you to call them to regain it or sell you a new one, which begins the cycle all over again.

Well, they categorically deny any such wrongdoing, of course. Instead, they offer this explanation: it's our fault. They even hire specialists to research the phenomenon. Here's what they've found:

People twist them by unconsciously following set patterns. For instance, when picking up the handset, many people turn it 90 degrees to put it under the left ear. After a while, they switch to the right ear, turning it a full 180 degrees. In order to hang it up so it sits correctly, it's easier to turn it another 90 degrees than go backwards 270 degrees. The result: one full twist. Repeat this often enough and you've got a cobra coil.

Other culprits: some people are actually "left-eared" but right-handed, or vice-versa; many people pace while chatting, leading to several twists in one call. There is a device called a "swivel," which acts much like the device that keeps a fishing line from twisting on a reel, but AT&T refused to market it, preferring, you guessed it, to just sell more new phones. The obvious solution: go cordless.

Why are queen-sized sheets always too small for queen-sized beds?

Inflation. It's not the sheet-makers' fault. The mattress manufacturers have run rampant in the last three decades trying to outdo each other in the *depth* of their mattresses. Length and width have remained standard since the early '60s, when the queen size expanded from 60 x 75 to 60 x 80. But no one has controlled the depth. In the early '80s, standard depth was seven inches. Now it's as much as 12 1/2 inches and still climbing. So, each year the sheet makers increase the length of their sheets (to cover the extra depth) by maybe an inch, hoping to at least keep up. Fat chance. They're still trying. A standard queen-size flat today is 90 x 102, which should suffice for a 60 x 80 bed. For awhile.

Why do electrical plugs have one blade wider than the other?

It's designed to be safer than the average older plug. They're protecting you from yourself. Without going into too much electrical mumbo-jumbo, the wide blade is "neutral" and the narrower blade is "hot." If you accidentally shoved a piece of metal into the hot side, you'd get jolted across the room, and might even get killed.

The primary reason for this safety improvement is to lesson the likelihood of touching the base of a light bulb, which is still visible even after it's screwed in, to the hot side. In the new plugs, all exposed electrical parts are neutralized. Sure, it's never happened in your life, what do you care? Well, it *could* have, and now it won't.

Why do light bulbs in lamps loosen after a long time, causing lit lights to suddenly lose luminescence?

All right, let's lose the ls. No, your house is not haunted by goblins who go around unscrewing light bulbs at inopportune moments, such as when you're soldering or sewing. It's the result of vibration. Over time, the threads that hold the bulb in place with friction are steadily overcome by vibrating sound or light waves. So, if you happen to like to play hard rock music at loud volumes, expect darkness in your life sooner than most.

How do refrigerators make food cold?

The Refrigerator Principle is the opposite of the Thermos Principle. To wit: whereas a Thermos keeps food cold by blocking heat from coming in, a refrigerator pushes heat *out*. If you doubt this, go feel the air behind your Coldspot.

The explanation is rather cumbersome, but suffice it to say that the cold liquid in the refrigerant (freon, in most cases) turns to a gas via electricity, and in so doing draws heat from the icebox. If you lick your finger and wave it in the air, it feels cooler for the same reason—as the liquid evaporates, heat is drawn into the air, leaving your finger colder. There's more to it than this, of course, but that's the idea that got the first refrigerator inventor to jump up and down excitedly.

Why does hot faucet water always come out strong, then slow to a trickle?

Things expand when they get warm, including rubber washers in water faucets. As the washer warms and expands, it gradually stifles the flow. You could take out the washer, but then your faucet might drip. Which would be worse? Thought so.

Why does water always drain out of the tub in a counterclockwise direction?

It's called the Coriolis effect, named after the French engineer who discovered it (or who was so bored he had nothing better to do than watch the water drain). The corollary to this is that in the Southern hemisphere, water drains clockwise.

Because the earth rotates, it exerts a force on things like water, which reacts according to laws of action and reaction and so forth. It has been proven time and again both north and south of the equator.

The force is not that strong, however, so it has no effect on larger bodies of water like oceans and rivers, or on stronger man-made forces like toilet flushes.

What's the best way to get rid of ants?

First, clean up. Leaving unwashed dishes, unswept floors, toaster crumbs, sugar spills, and other insect goodies exposed are clarion calls for the ant brigade. Doing this on a regular basis should cure your problem. If you do insist on living an Oscar Madison lifestyle, try ant sticks. These are stakes that stick in the ground outside and divert the troops from their route, leaving the inside of your home fresh and ant-free. For errant soldiers and trail scouts, try leaving bay leaves around the ant entry hole. Ants hate bay leaves. If all else fails, scream at them. They'll think you're insane, and this will upset their fine sense of order and cause them to retreat.

Food and Drink

What happens when you swallow chewing gum? Does it really stick to your ribs?

Gum is not food. Therefore, gum cannot be digested. There are too many acids in your stomach to just let it hang out there unperturbed, or, heaven forbid, adhere itself to a rib like a barnacle. It's a wet environment down there—things just flow through. So, gum goes where every other non-food item goes: out the other end.

Why is American beer so wimpy?

We big, strong, burly Americans *like* our beer weak and watery. Why? We've been trained that way.

Despite the presence of richer, more flavorful European beers, 95% of domestically-consumed beer is brewed right here. There are several reasons for our extreme loyalty.

First, we like to chug. Darker, richer beers are heavier and more filling. You can't chug them as well as you can a beer that's mostly carbonated water, with a few hops and yeast thrown in. Frat parties demand good chugging.

Second, the realities of the marketplace determined that lighter, cheaper, more "drinkable" beer would sell better, and people would buy more of it. Of course, the most drinkable substance is water, and high water content adds to enormous profits.

Third, American beer companies train their young. Most advertising campaigns are targeted at 16-year-olds, believe it or not. Okay, bikini-clad fantasy babes, rock and roll, short-attention-span cuts—*now* you believe it. Since, presumably, a 16-year-old kid is innocent in the ways of beer, he thinks these commercials are cool. By the time he's 18, he chooses his favorite. Studies show that once he's chosen his brand, he's *extremely* loyal—it's part of his identity. So once they got you, they can count on you, and go after your little brother.

How does Campbell's Soup decide which letters to put in their alphabet soup? What are these letters made out of?

You know, there's the broth, the vegetables, and the, uh, letters. Macaroni, you say? Isn't macaroni a form of pasta? Doesn't pasta require at least a *little* chewing? You certainly don't chew the letters—they're just *there*.

They are indeed macaroni, albeit a bleached-out, extremely soggy version of it. All that time sitting in a can of broth, one supposes. As for letter distribution, that appears to be quite random: all 26 letters are distributed equally and without purpose. There are two sizes, though—small letters tend to go into ready-to-eat soups like the Chunky line; larger letters are in the standard condensed soup cans, such as the vegetable varieties.

How can you tell a poisonous wild mushroom from a safe one?

You can't, at least not until you eat it. By then, of course, you could be dead. But there are mushroom specialists—professionals and amateurs—who study the nuances and know what to look for. Mushrooms sold in the supermarket are, of course, quite harmless—they're grown on special edible mushroom farms. But don't ever eat a wild one unless you absolutely know what you're doing—it really could kill you.

Why are mustard bottles short and round while ketchup bottles are tall and skinny?

It's due to a difference in pungency. Mustard has a sharp bite to it, so you don't need a lot of it. You tend to scoop out only as much as you need with a knife, and that's easily accomplished if the jar is round and squat, so it keeps its balance while you scoop.

Ketchup, however, is relatively spice-less. It's just a blandish tomato variation. So go ahead and heap it on. Since it's essentially a liquid, heaping it is as good as pouring, and pouring is best done with a narrow spout.

More Important Question Number One: Why did it take so long for ketchup makers to switch from glass bottles to plastic "easy pour" bottles? Alas, after years of shaking the bottle, slapping the bottom, tapping a knife to the edge, and other creative jump-starts, the fine art of ketchup coaxing appears to have sadly become lost.

More Important Question Number Two: What about those industrial-strength mustard and ketchup dispensers at ballparks? Can't we use *those* at home? Yes, you could, but no one sells the stuff in those containers, and admit it, you're too lazy to transfer it. Why bother? And who consumes condiments to that degree in the home, anyway?

Why do people still insist on giving fruitcakes for Christmas when we all hate them?

You've no doubt heard the joke that there is only one fruitcake in the world—people just keep giving it away.

The practice apparently started—and still exists—because fruitcake makers sell mostly to civic clubs (Rotary, Kiwanis, Elks, Moose, that sort of thing), who sell them door-to-door as fund-raisers. Their victims are charitable do-gooders who figure they'll just give the thing to that aunt they don't really know, or that hard-to-buy-for father-in-law. Soon, we're swimming in hard, impenetrable red-and-green-dyed glucose matter.

Why did all the clubs choose fruitcakes to sell? Evidently one zealous salesman in Tampa in the early '50s quite liked the stuff, so he turned all his buddies onto it. It also helps that its shelf life is 120 to 150 days—that's four to five months at room temperature, longer still if you refrigerate it. And even if you don't, just give it away next year. No one actually eats it anymore. It's like a chain letter—people are afraid of what might happen if they don't pass it on.

How did doughnuts come to have holes?

The origin of the doughnut is a hotly-debated topic among those in the baking industry. We do know that virtually every culture has enjoyed a form of fried cake. The Dutch are credited with popularizing them in colonial America. In New York, for instance, they were called dough nuts because they were served as round balls of sweetened dough, fried in hog fat. In the late 17th century doughnuts were so popular that shops sprang up serving them with coffee (could this be the oldest true American "meal?").

One story persists about the hole. Seems a sea captain named Hanson Gregory was enjoying a fried cake while steering his ship one night (again, the similarity to modern-day usage is chilling: we do this every morning in rush-hour traffic). A storm hit, the ship started rocking, and Gregory needed both hands to steer, so he instinctively jammed the fritter over one of the wheel's spokes. Et voila. Delighted with the handiness of his new creation, he instructed his cook to make more that way.

Why doesn't it help to swallow water when your mouth is burning with spicy food?

Once again, it all comes down to one of life's essential truths: oil and water don't mix. Most hot spices are oil-based, so water just flows right past them. What you need is something to soak up the oil.

The best solution: bread, or the nearest available starch, say, a tortilla chip. Savor the bread, roll it around in there awhile, soak up the hot stuff. Next-best solution: milk. Although milk is water-based, it contains a detergent-like ingredient that combines with the oil (like soap does) and washes it out.

Last resort: tequila. Any liquor will dissolve the oil, but it will also plaster you.

How long can you store a potato?

Used to be a freshly-dug potato would only keep for a few months before the eyes began to sprout (do not eat those). Now, they'll last as long as three years because of a synthetic spray—just wash them before you eat them.

Most other vegetables perish more quickly, but scientists are working on it.

What's the best way to keep soda from going flat?

Drink it chilled right out of the can—or bottle, as the case may be. Do not pour room temperature soda into a glass filled with ice to chill it—the poor carbonation molecules will be shocked into submission by the radical temperature change, and the drink will automatically lose about 50% of its fizziness. If you're the type of a person that simply must drink out of a glass, then pour a refrigerated soda into a chilled container—that way you lose only about 10% of the fizz on impact, and the rest stays bubbly a bit longer.

Interestingly, the amount of carbonation in soft drinks varies little between brands, but it does vary significantly between flavor types. On the low side, fruit flavors like orange and grape sodas are the flattest, then comes root beer, cola, and lemon-lime. The fizziest? Ginger ale. So that's why grandma always prescribed it for upset stomachs.

Why did Coca-Cola change to New Coke a few years ago? Whatever happened to New Coke?

In the '80s, Pepsi was gaining on Coke, even though the latter always had the larger market share. Taste tests showed more people preferred the sweeter Pepsi. So Coke started to panic: they called R&D and ordered them to experiment. After much mixing and stirring, they found their grand new formula, and were elated when, in every blindfold test, New Coke outscored old Coke. Finally, the corporate brass said, "What the heck?" and went for it.

You know the rest. It was one of the biggest blunders of modern civilization. People were so outraged that Coke had changed the formula they refused to touch the new stuff, taste tests and Bill Cosby's entreaties be damned. We were all hooked on the old stuff, had sentimental memories associated with it and whatnot. Either that or underneath, we're all just trained monkeys.

Why does sour cream have an expiration date?

Hmmm. It's already sour . . . Can it get any more, er, sour? Well, yes, actually. Sour cream can only last about a month in the refrigerator before it begins to taste, you know, funny. Bacteria begins to take over, then it becomes downright dangerous. Moldy even. We don't recommend it. Degrees of sourness, it seems, are relative.

Why is cheddar cheese orange?

Because cows produce orange milk, of course. Uh, okay. Milk is white, cheese is white. Yet we Americans seem to like our cheese orange. It makes it more appetizing. The folks at Kraft have tested white cheese in the marketplace, but it doesn't sell. So they artificially color it using natural ingredients like annatto, a seed from a Central American tree, and oleoresin paprika. By blending these in, they can dye it any shade of yellow or orange they wish.

Why do we call a hamburger a "hamburger," when clearly it does not contain ham?

The hamburger was not named for the meat it contains, but for the city that popularized it—Hamburg, Germany.

The obvious question now is, are there towns in Germany called Cheeseburg, Steakburg, Baconburg, or Happyburg? For that matter, is there a town in England called Fishwhich?

What days of the year is it possible to stand an egg on its end?

Your correspondent was very impressed one March 21st when a friend's wise father demonstrated his ability to stand an egg on its end. He proclaimed that this could only be done on this particular day, the vernal equinox, when the sun passes directly over the equator, thus making day and night the same length, and presumably, gravitational forces perfectly balanced.

You know what? He was wrong. Try it. You can do it anytime. It just takes a little practice and the right egg. One tip: shake the egg first. That will break the yolk loose from the little stringy bands that hold it in place in the center. That way, it will settle on the bottom, making the egg bottom-heavy and giving you a successful party trick.

Why do wintergreen Life Savers make blue sparks when you bite them in the dark?

Another groovy party trick. Grab a roll, turn the lights out, bite down and impress your friends with a blue-green fireworks display in your mouth. What gives?

It's the result of a chemical combination of the mint flavoring and crystalline sugar. Cracking it releases the compound's potential energy, which results in the laser show.

Experimentation has shown the trick to be most effective in very dark, very dry rooms, so don't try it in a steamy, well-lit bathroom.

How did 7UP get its name?

An entrepreneur in St. Louis named C.L. Grigg had already had success with his first soft drink, Howdy Orange, in the 1920s. Seeking another score, he tried several formulas for lemon, then finally hit on a combination of seven natural flavors—hence the name (even though we think of it as a lemon-lime drink).

The soda was first promoted as a healthy tonic—to "energize the muscles . . . soothe the nerves . . . and make your body alive," which is another reason why grandma still gives it to you for tummy aches.

Furthermore, its success was due partially to the ingenious name, which became a part of the American vocabulary. When each team in a football game has scored a touchdown, for instance, we commonly say that the score is "seven up."

Who is Dr. Pepper and why does he have a soft drink?

This, friends, is a story of unrequited love, the story of a broken heart that launched the nation's longest-surviving soft drink brand.

Dr. Charles Pepper owned a drug store in a small town in Virginia, and his underling pharmacist, Wade Morrison, fell in love with the doctor's daughter. When he found out, Pepper was peeved. He kicked Wade out of town, so the young pharmacist moved to Waco, Texas and opened his own place, Morrison's Old Corner Drug Store.

Morrison in turn hired an assistant pharmacist, Charles Alderton, to help fill orders and tend the soda fountain. After awhile, Alderton noticed the fruit-flavored soft drinks just weren't moving, so on a slow day in 1885, he played around with the syrups, and mixed them up into a whole new blend. Folks started asking for it. Even the morose Morrison enjoyed it.

The new concoction needed a name, so one of the patrons, hearing about Morrison's sad story, jokingly suggested naming it Dr. Pepper to placate the old man. Who knows, maybe it would help win back the girl.

And so it was.

Word of the drink spread far and wide. Other stores began ordering the syrup. In 1904, it was introduced to the rest of the world at the St. Louis World's Fair, along with such novel treats as the ice cream cone, the hamburger, and the hot dog.

Morrison got rich, and perhaps some measure of revenge, but he never got his girl. Alderton, the drink's actual creator, never involved himself in the Dr. Pepper company, and just continued to fill prescriptions.

If you're toasting a single slice of bread, what happens when you put it in the side of the toaster not marked "single slice?"

This is, of course, a felony, much like removing the tag of a mattress. If everyone ignored these little laws, total chaos would ensue, society as we know it would fall apart, and mankind would probably end up destroying itself. All because you *had* to break the rules.

Okay, here's the answer: the toaster's thermostat is in the "single slice" slot. So if your bread happens to be in the other slot, it will conceivably toast forever, since the silly contraption would never know when it's time to pop up. Then again, the toaster used for this research never pops up anyway—we toast the old-fashioned way here, *by feel*. In fact, it seems that's the way most toasters end up, so in the end it doesn't matter which side you're on, so to speak, because you're probably used to popping it up yourself.

Is it possible to pop regular corn kernels? What makes popcorn different?

There's a little science to this popcorn stuff, so bear with us. Of the five types of corn, only popcorn pops on a consistent basis. It is possible that the others will pop occasionally, but it's so seldom that it's pointless to force it. They're just not made for it.

The key is water content. The ideal level is about 13.5% in each kernel. When the water is heated, it expands, pressing on the hard outer starch of the kernel until it explodes, turning it inside out. The water is released in the form of steam (that's why you should always stand back when you open a package of the stuff after nuking it—it comes out like an overheated radiator), and the soft inner starch is what's left—and what's so fun to eat. Remember when it used to be "more fun to make than it is to eat?" Ah, microwaves.

If you ate nothing but carrots, would you turn orange?

Like a pumpkin. In fact, we have observed this first-hand in our research. A friend would take beta carotene vitamins—lots of them—every day, so his hands, arms, face, everything—was orange. It was a bit frightening.

Carotene is the key ingredient here, the very same vitamin that gives carrots its pigment (and you, if you have a nice orange suit and shoes to match). Perhaps our friend was a little enthusiastic in his dosage. It needn't be so. A normal amount of carotene is great for you—it's a prime combatant of cancer, and is also found in broccoli, squash, and cantaloupe.

As for the old adage that carrots improve your eyesight, that, unfortunately, has never been proven.

Science

What makes the sky blue? The sun yellow? The ocean blue? Sunsets reddish-orange?

Believe it or not, there's one answer for all these questions. First of all, the sun emits every color all at once, which results in plain old white. But when it hits our atmosphere, strange things happen. Each color gets separated, bent, and scattered all over the place, because each has a different frequency, or wave length (this is where it gets complicated).

The frequency that best travels straight on through the ozone layer is yellow, so that's why the sun looks yellow to us. Of the other colors, blue is scattered around to the sides the most, thus making the sky appear blue. If it weren't this way, our "yellow" sun would appear against a black sky, like on the moon, where there is no atmosphere.

The ocean is made of water, which of course is naturally colorless. But underneath, it's rather dense, so light doesn't pass through it too well; instead, it bounces back up. Most of the day, the sky is blue, so the ocean just sits there bouncing that blue light back up to us. (On gray days, of course, it appears much darker.)

When the sun goes down, most of its rays travel to our eyes lengthwise, or horizontally, rather than vertically. At this stage of the scattering process, red-orange light travels best, so the sun looks fiery-red to us.

Does a full moon affect people's behavior?

Some guys turn into werewolves. Others reportedly get a bit punchier—one study of British soccer fans claimed they got rowdier during full moons. Nurses and cops claim their business always goes up on full-moon nights. Supposedly, even traffic accidents increase.

The reasoning? They say that when the moon is full, it exerts a greater gravitational pull on our bodies; since we're mostly water, it's as if our tides are highest that night.

Is there any proof of this? None whatsoever. In fact, it's complete bunko. The study of traffic accidents was disproved due to the fact that full moons tended to happen on the weekends when the study was conducted; traffic accidents always rise on the weekends because everybody's out drinking and partying. The soccer study was not taken seriously mainly because British soccer fans are *always* rowdy.

The tidal-pull theory is meaningless for two reasons: first, tides occur once or twice a day, not once a month, so theoretically we should feel mood swings accordingly (perhaps *that's* worth studying); second, the main reason the moon appears full is due to lighting—in that position, the greatest amount of the sun's light is reflected by it. The effect of its gravitational pull due to alignment is quite negligible.

The fact is, crazy things happen everyday. But when the moon is full, it's convenient to say, "Oh look, it's a full moon—*that's* why that guy keeps staring at me funny." All the other days of the month lack the easy out, and rightly so. We're always looking for simple answers to perplexing questions, and usually there's more to it than that.

Why can't we see the "dark side" of the moon?

Because it doesn't rotate. It makes a complete orbit of the earth every twenty-nine-and-a-half days, but it doesn't spin like we do.

For example, imagine you are the moon and your friend Dusty is the earth. Ask Dusty to turn around and around for awhile. Now walk all the way around him using sideways steps. He never sees the back of your head, does he?

We have pictures of the back of the moon. Russians first shot them on a trip in the '60s (then invited their friends Igor and Natasha over to watch the slides and play pinochle). It's a little smoother than the face we know and love—sort of like the man in the moon has a bald noggin.

Why does the wind blow?

Because the sun is warm. Simple, right? Here's how it works.

The sun heats the air in certain places—say, the equator, where the distance between the sun and the earth is usually the shortest. Warm air rises. It's less dense than cool air, because heat excites molecules to fly around really fast; cold air makes molecules squeeze tightly together. So, when the warm air vacates its spot, cool air rushes in to replace it—there always has to be air in our atmosphere. This cool air usually comes from the north and south, creating wind. The warm air is in turn blown around to the north and south, where it eventually meets cooler air (creating a storm), cools off and sinks back down, beginning the cycle all over again.

Why can't we drink ocean water?

Because it's too salty. The body needs to maintain just the right balance of water to salt. If you eat salty foods, you get real thirsty. If you lose salt through vigorous exercise, a flavored drink like Gatorade becomes mighty tempting, because it replaces some lost sodium in addition to the water.

But the salt content in the ocean is so high, it would just make you thirstier for pure water. If you drank more ocean water as a result, you'd be thirstier still, until eventually you died of thirst.

Someday in the future, perhaps desalinization machines will become small and portable, making the need to carry fresh water on boating trips obsolete.

Is there a possibility that a large asteroid will crash into the earth, killing us off like the one that wiped out the dinosaurs?

About 67 million years ago, an asteroid about five miles wide appears to have smashed into the ground near Manson, Iowa, creating a cloud of dust that darkened the planet for months (probably caused quite a ruckus among the prehistoric clanfolk of Manson as well—for the local Fred Flintstones, it was suddenly bowling night—every night). The lack of photosynthesis killed most of the vegetation, which in turn starved two-thirds of the animals on the planet, including Dino.

If it happened now, of course, *we'd* be history, too. The chances of one that size hitting us are extremely remote, but hey, anything is possible. It's a big, fat, unpredictable universe out there. But it is more likely that a smaller one will eventually cross our path. In fact, in 1989, we had a near-miss (who knew?). An asteroid the size of three football fields was traveling at 20 miles *per second*—that's 72,000 miles per hour—and missed us by six hours and half a million miles (a close call by astronomical standards). If it had hit us, it would have had the force of 20,000 hydrogen bombs—a real nuclear winter, and not even by our own hand.

This prompts another question: could we destroy another similar flying rock with a nuclear defense system before it hits us? Well, we might not hit a bullseye, but we could probably divert it. Problem is, it's dark, and we might not see it against that black universe backdrop until it entered our atmosphere. By then, it could be too late—at 20 miles per second, we'd have to act incredibly fast.

Would it burn up when it hit our atmosphere? Small ones do all the time. In fact, our little ozone layer is our best defense—that's exactly what it's for. Now, as long as we don't erode it by manufacturing more Styrofoam, hair spray, and air conditioners, we should be all right.

How many stars are there in the universe? What is the probability of life outside our solar system?

In our galaxy, the Milky Way, there are about 100 billion stars. That we know of. In addition to that, there are at least a billion other *galaxies*. That we know of. Each, like ours, potentially contains at least 100 billion stars. This is to say nothing about each of those stars entertaining a family of planets of their own. Want to go further?

If only a fraction of those megazillions of planets out there has, like Earth, the necessary ingredients for life—you know, carbon, nitrogen, hydrogen, oxygen, that sort of thing—the probability of extra-terrestrial life is indeed overwhelming. You can just take it to the bank. We are not alone. It's inconceivable that with all those stars and planets and, who knows, *universes* out there that we are the only ones. That's what makes Star Trek and other science fiction entertaining—it's relatively believable, in theory.

Why do stars twinkle?

For the same reason the wind blows: warm air rises. Just as you can see air dancing above hot pavement, so hot air in the atmosphere is bent back and forth by wind forces. Between this and all the dust in the atmosphere, starlight appears to twinkle because of all this bending to and fro.

Will the sun ever burn out?

Sure, but not for awhile. It's not like a campfire log, which burns out relatively quickly due to its breathing oxygen. Our sun does not inhale. Never did, never will (that's why it's the boss).

The Sun is a nuclear fusion reactor. That is to

say, at its core, hydrogen atoms that normally repel each other are fused together to form helium. What strange force pushes the little buggers into this matrimony? Blame it on the Big Bang—that huge burst of energy is still feeding the universe on its momentum. Anyway, the resulting explosion releases enormous amounts of thermal energy, a tiny fraction of which ultimately sustains life as we know it here.

And since it's not breathing oxygen, it's a far more efficient burner. By the time it peters out, a few billion years will have passed, and so will everything we know.

Can two snowflakes ever be alike?

Yep. Problem is, the likelihood of ever finding these twins is purdy slim—you have to look real hard. One scientist discovered two identical snow "crystals" recently while browsing—they weren't flakes per se, but they prove the point.

What is an iceberg?

A mountain of pure ice, or a very unpleasant person. In parts of the world where even summer is cold, snow never melts. It just keeps piling on top of itself. Thus, a glacier is born. Eventually, heavy pressure causes a piece to break off—water from a nearby ocean helps soften it a bit. It just floats right down into the sea. Like an island, it's a huge mass that only pokes its head out on top of the water—there's much more underneath. If only the captain of the Titanic had realized this.

Does hot water freeze faster than cold water?

Not exactly. This is another misbegotten wives' tale. Mildly cold water—say about 40 degrees—will freeze faster than mildly hot water (125 degrees). *But,* very hot water (195+) will freeze faster than mildly hot water.

Why? Because near the boiling point, heat escapes quickly, shrinking the volume. So less water means faster boiling. Also, the very fact that the hot molecules are escaping so quickly means that slower, colder ones are left behind. Thus, the evaporation process itself is a boon to the freezing process. Weird, but true.

Will the earth ever get sucked into a black hole?

Black holes are incredibly fascinating, but we'll never get to experience one, unless Universal Studios comes up with a new ride that approximates it (hey—what a great idea!). Our sun is just too small to ever become one.

Scientists believe black holes used to be former very large stars that are now in their final stage of evolution. After they expanded to great size, their gases burned out and they began to collapse back into themselves by gravitational pull. In fact, the force of a black hole is so strong that it sucks everything into its vortex—including light. We know it's there because we can see other objects orbiting around a center where no light exists.

What would happen if you fell into one? First, you'd be ripped apart instantaneously, because the pull on one end of you would be much stronger than the pull on the other end. You'd also be exposed to massive radiation.

But let's just imagine you were somehow wearing an amazing tidal-proof, radiation-proof suit. What then? After spinning wildly into the vortex (like those guys in the old "Time Tunnel" TV series), it's possible that there could be an "other end" that you could be spit out of.

What's on the other side? A different universe? Our anti-universe, where everything is the opposite of what we know? Time travel?

Could be. Seriously—all of the above is possible. Einstein proved that if you could travel at the speed of light, you would indeed be timeless yourself. You would never age. Since the gravitational pull of a black hole is *stronger* than the speed of light, it's possible that through it, we can travel *back in time*. Or glimpse a whole new universe, of different dimensions, or even our exact opposites. It's great to still have a frontier like this that we'll never get to explore, so have fun wondering. And you thought those science fiction guys were wacko.

American History

Who was the first president of the United States?

Ha. You think you know this one, but you'd be surprised. George Washington was actually the first elected president in 1789, but if you want to be particular, the office actually originated eight years before that.

Between 1781 and 1789, eight men presided over the Continental Congress in Philadelphia, the first being John Hanson, whose official title was "president of the United States in Congress assembled." Hanson's main achievement? Prior to becoming president, he served in the Maryland assembly for twenty years, then convinced his home state, which was the only one opposing the Articles of Confederation, to approve them, thus ensuring the adoption of the constitution. Not bad for a "nobody."

Did Betsy Ross really sew the American flag?

No, nor did she design it. That credit belongs to Francis Hopkinson, a naval designer who was commissioned but never paid for his work. The Betsy Ross tale was originated by her grandson, William J. Canby, in 1870, who charmed the Pennsylvania Historical Society with an anecdote about how George Washington and two senior officials wandered into Betsy's Philadelphia seamstress shop and asked her to sew their design. The society loved it, felt proud that one of their own had contributed so humbly to the young nation, and soon all the textbooks treated it as gospel. But there is absolutely no evidence to support it. All we know for sure is that Betsy sewed some flags for the Pennsylvania navy in 1777.

Was turkey actually served at the first Thanksgiving?

Nope. The actual menu consisted of venison, duck, goose, seafood, eels, corn bread, various greens, berries, and wine. And even though the feast was first held in 1621, it wasn't an annual event; instead it was more of a sporadic celebration held after a particularly bountiful harvest or a battle victory. It took Sarah Josepha Hale, the editor of Ladies' Magazine, thirty six years to finally win her campaign to make it a national holiday in 1863.

Did native Americans really sell Manhattan for $24?

Yes. Peter Minuit bought the island from the leaders of the Manhattoe tribe for a package of cloth and trinkets of roughly that value.

How did California get its name?

No, it isn't Spanish for "granola" or "tummy tuck" or "skateboard." In 1535, the Spanish conqueror Cortez had a vision. As he was sailing by a finger of land, it reminded him of an imaginary island in a popular Spanish novel he'd been reading. The island's ruler was a black-skinned female named Calafia. Seven years later, when Cabrillo followed, he found the entire coastline named California—and freeways everywhere.

Were witches burnt at Salem?

No, but nineteen young girls were hanged and one male "witch" was pressed to death under heavy weights for refusing to plea. The actual number of deaths has long been exaggerated, due to the public's fascination with the subject.

What really happened? Were the girls "possessed?" Historians suggest it was a confluence of several factors at once: First, the town's religious leaders needed—and used—the opportunity to strengthen their authority, so they did so by casting out these "demons" to "save" their town; second, a convincing argument can be made that a sort of "craze" was started among the teenagers by one girl's dysfunctional ploy for attention, and it simply got out of hand and was badly misdiagnosed and misinterpreted; third, social analysts point out the underpinnings of a class conflict between the girls' families and their persecutors. No one knows for sure, however, and the episode remains a compelling mystery.

How was the great Chicago fire started?

Okay, so everybody loves the cute story of Mrs. O'Leary's cow kicking over a lantern, setting fire to its straw, then its barn, then the city. And everyone knows it's a tall tale. A reporter later admitted to making up the story because it seemed colorful, and it boosted circulation. Ah, journalism . . .

Chicago had actually had several small fires in the days before the big one, prompting the Tribune to caution that "a spark might set a fire which would sweep from end to end of the city." On October 8, 1871, it did, destroying 17,000 buildings in the downtown area and causing about $200 million of damage. 500 people were reported dead or missing.

The fire was traceable to the household of Patrick and Catherine O'Leary, who were having friends over that night for a round of cards, but all involved denied any carelessness with lanterns or cigars. The only culprit left to blame, then, was the cow.

While we're on the subject of natural disasters, the 1906 San Francisco earthquake was the most severe in American history, right?

Wrong, in a sense. It did cause the most damage, in terms of lives and property, but its Richter scale measurement of 8.3 places it second in intensity. The winner? On December 16, 1811, a quake in Missouri, of all places, would have registered 8.7 (had there been measurements taken then), but due to the paucity of its population, the effects of the disruption were experienced mostly by the natural flora and fauna. So it ain't just California that's shaking, folks.

Why is "The Star Spangled Banner" our national anthem, and not "America the Beautiful?"

Because we Americans love challenges, and the "Banner" is a much more difficult song to sing—especially those second, third, and fourth verses (how many of us know them?). One other note: Francis Scott Key did not compose the song, he just wrote the lyrics. The music is actually from an 18th-century drinking song by British composer John Stafford Smith called "To Anacreon"—it's an homage to a Greek poet who loved wine and women. Remember that the next time you're at a ball game with a beer in your hand.

Did Prohibition abolish drinking?

No. Just the "manufacture, sale, or transportation" of liquor. Conceivably, you could be caught stone drunk between 1920 and 1933 and be completely innocent, because you didn't make it, sell it, or move it—you just drank it. Hey, you didn't think the Roaring Twenties, with all that hot jazz music and jitterbugging and flappering, was created by sober people, did you?

Was Abraham Lincoln assassinated by John Wilkes Booth?

We all thought we knew this one. Yes, Booth did fire the shot in Ford's Theater in 1865. But he wasn't acting alone. In fact, he was part of a larger plot to overthrow the entire government—Vice President Andrew Johnson and Secretary of State William Seward were to be killed as well. Booth's accomplice Lewis Paine shot Seward the same night as the Lincoln assassination, but Seward survived.

In fact, several conspirators, including former Confederacy president Jefferson Davis, were implicated, and four were hanged amid public protests of unfair trials. One of those four was Mary Surratt, who became the first woman in U.S. history so executed. Former actor Booth was cornered on a Virginia farm twelve days after the assassination, and either shot himself or was killed by the rather unstable Boston Corbett, who claimed God told him to pull the trigger (Corbett later castrated himself, then shot up the Kansas legislature and was committed; he later escaped).

Some historians have suggested that the mastermind was actually Secretary of War Edwin Stanton, who perhaps had attempted to kidnap Lincoln because of his opposition to reconstruction. In any case, much like the Kennedy assassination, the more you look the weirder it gets, and the less absolute the answers become.

Assassination Question Number Two: Kennedy. Who? How? Why? Does anyone alive know? Castro? Oliver Stone?

It's all so dizzying. But here are the facts as reported to us by Congress after two years of investigation:

1) A panel of forensic pathologists reviewed the autopsy photos of Kennedy's head. Overwhelming conclusion (one dissenter): he was shot from the back. Implication: Lee Harvey Oswald shot him alone (i.e., there was no evidence of a "grassy knoll" shooter from the front).

2) Obviously, Castro had a motive—the CIA had attempted to overthrow him; so did the Mafia—Attorney General Robert Kennedy had been cracking down on them. Oswald was a Castro/communist sympathizer, while Jack Ruby (who

killed Oswald) had mob ties. Sounds too perfect to be true, right? Seems so. More evidence suggests the improbability of a conspiracy: Oswald, for instance, was not a plant in the Texas School Book Depository, because he was already employed there *before* Kennedy's advisers planned their route, and no evidence has ever implicated Kennedy's aides. Plus, neither Oswald nor Ruby were "professionals"—they were both proven losers, not exactly the type serious conspirators hire for an important hit. Even Ruby's shooting was a weird accident of circumstance, since he casually arrived an hour late to Oswald's scheduled transfer from the police station, only to find that the transfer itself had been delayed an hour. Real hit men aren't late to a job, and aren't so nonchalant.

There's more, but you get the drift. The fact as best we know them seem clearly supportive of the lone gunman theory. But, hey, where's the mystery in accepting that?

How did the feud between the Hatfields and the McCoys get started?

In 1882, a McCoy killed a Hatfield. No one remembers why. For the next 28 years, each revenge begat another. This all happened across the Tug Fork River in the Appalachian Mountains—the Hatfields lived in Logan County, West Virginia, and the McCoys in Pike County, Kentucky. Kin will be kin.

What really happened at the O.K. Corral?

On October 26, 1881, in Tombstone, Arizona, the three Earp brothers—Wyatt, Virgil, and Morgan—along with their buddy Doc Holliday, each of whom had a bad reputation, shot Billy Clanton and Tom and Frank McLaury. Much like the Hatfields and McCoys, there were serious family disputes here, and evidence shows the Earps and Holliday shot the others without provocation. They were later cleared.

Where did the word "okay" come from?

There are several theories here. Pick any one you like.

1. The Choctaw Indian word for "yes" is "okeh."

2. A railroad freight agent named Obedieh Kelly used to stamp his initials on papers to show they were approved and in order.

3. There was a port in Haiti called Aux Cayes, which is of course pronounced "okay." Sailors loved to frequent it because of its high quality of rum, so they supposedly began referring to anything they liked as "Aux Cayes stuff."

4. A Columbia University professor claims that the term derived from "oll korrect," which was a

jokingly-spelled version of "all correct."

5. In 1840, when Martin Van Buren was running for president, he was nicknamed "Old Kinderhook," after his New York hometown. His campaign supporters called themselves "The OK Club," and shouted "OK" at rallies. After he won, the whole country was familiar with the term, and used it to mean "all right" from then on.

Were people actually ever tarred and feathered?

Well, it beat being hanged, although not by much. Mobs tarred and feathered their prey when they were feeling less vicious than playful. The victim was stripped naked, covered with hot tar, then coated with feathers or any odd assortment of embarrassing decorations that happened to be nearby. Victims usually survived, but the smelly black stuff often left bad blisters and scars, and took hours to scrape off with turpentine. The practice seems to have ended just after the turn of the century, although some fraternity hazing practices often resemble it.

Who was the original Uncle Sam?

No one really knows, but many believe he was a meat packer from Troy, New York named Sam Wilson, who worked for Elbert Anderson, a ration supplier to the U.S. Army in the War of 1812.

As the story goes, all the company's meat was stamped "E.A.—U.S.," presumably for "Elbert Anderson—United States." But Wilson used to joke that the "U.S." stood for "Uncle Sam," referring to himself. What a riot those meat packers can be.

Problem is, nobody in Troy—not even the local newspapers—had ever heard this story, although they knew Sam. But faraway reporters knew it, which suggests that it was another folksy tale somebody just made up. Ain't it always the way.

The nickname was popularized by newspapers who opposed the country's involvement in the War of 1812. Later, in the 1820s, the famous cartoonist Thomas Nast—who also created the image of the Republican elephant, popularized the Democratic donkey, and first drew Santa Claus as a fat man in a red suit—fixed the image of Uncle Sam as tall and thin, with a white beard and top hat.

In 1961, Congress passed a resolution recognizing Sam Wilson as the original Uncle Sam.

How were the Republican elephant and Democratic donkey created?

In the 1828 election, democrat Andrew Jackson's opponents called him a "jackass." Jackson mocked them by using it as his symbol, and it stuck. Cartoonist Thomas Nast, after popularizing the donkey, invented the elephant in 1874 to represent the Republican party's immense strength at the time.

The Battle of New Orleans ended the War of 1812, right?

Not really. You see, the battle took place *after* the war had ended. This may come as a cold shock to those Americans who view it as a patriotic symbol of glory.

After British naval forces were defeated on September 14, 1814 on Lake Champlain, the Brits signed a peace treaty, ending the war on Christmas Eve of that year. Unfortunately, the mail was slow in those days. In mid-January, Andrew Jackson's troops killed two thousand British soldiers, only to discover in February that they had done so in peacetime.

Why is "Remember the Alamo" such a treasured battle cry?

It's not because the loss was noble. Ostensibly fighting for "independence," Texas settlers simply preferred American rule over Mexican authority, mostly because America would let them keep their slaves (although, to be fair, the Mexican government was renowned for its cruelty and corruption).

Of course, colorful characters like Jim Bowie

and Davy Crockett add to its mystique, as does good-old American underdog sympathy—less than two hundred rag-tag defenders killed over fifteen hundred Mexican soldiers. Makes for a great movie, but in reality, it was not all good guys and bad guys. Even the decision to fight is questionable: The conflict could have been easily avoided if Sam Houston's orders to abandon the fortress had been followed. Sorry, folks, but "Remember the Alamo" could stand for futility and selfishness as much as it does for against-all-odds heroism and honor.

Why did General Custer press on into an un-winnable battle?

Because he was an idiot. It's true. Once again, the movies doth lie. Before his demise, he was known as an arrogant hot-head who led daredevil charges in the Civil War, then was court-martialed once for disobeying orders. His greed even led him to massacre Native American camps in search of gold. As for his Little Big Horn defeat, he decided to ignore his superior's battle plan and take Sitting Bull's hidden camp by himself. This required splitting his forces into three columns, which led to the rout of each by an overwhelming number of Cheyenne and Sioux warriors. By the way, Custer wasn't even a general—he had lost that title after the Civil War—but a lieutenant colonel.

Ironically, although it was the Indians' greatest victory, it triggered their ultimate demise. White Americans were so outraged by the news that they rose up in greater numbers and defeated the Indians a few years later.

Could the U.S. have prevented or lessened the damage in the Pearl Harbor attack?

On the morning of December 7, 1941, ten hours before the attack, a 14-part Japanese message was intercepted by Americans and decoded at 4:37 A.M. Washington time. Unfortunately, it remained in the code room for another three hours, when it was delivered to President Roosevelt. At 11 A.M., the army and navy began transmitting the message to all bases in the Pacific *except* Hawaii, because its receiver was not working. Pearl Harbor finally got the message three hours after the attack, which cost 3,000 lives.

World History

Was Bohemia a real country? How did it come to signify a creative lifestyle?

Bohemia was originally located in what is now the Czech Republic. It was founded in the tenth century, ruled by Austria from 1526 to 1914, and at the end of World War I, joined with Moravia and Slovakia to form Czechoslovakia.

The French believed that Gypsies came from Bohemia, and since artists often led vagabondish, Gypsy-like lives in their creative pursuits, they were soon called "Bohemians." Appropriately, one of today's most popular travel destinations for free-thinking college students and artists is Prague, located in the former Bohemia.

Did the Hundred Years' War last a hundred years?

Well, the Thirty Years' War lasted thirty years (1618-1648), and the Seven Years' War lasted seven years (1756-1763), but when it comes to such a big number, why not just round off? The Hundred Years' War took place from 1337-1453. That's 116 years altogether, but who's counting. You could even say it lasted 138 years if you're really picky and only acknowledge the peace treaty in 1475.

Basically, it was a war of egos between England and France, who duked it out over a small piece of French land called Guienne. It did provide a wealth of material for Shakespeare, who used it as a great metaphor for man's inhumanity to man, greed, arrogance, and such, with characters such as Edward the Black Prince and Richard III. So, it indirectly served as a valuable lesson for those of us who choose to remember the past so that we don't repeat it, as the saying goes. Oh yeah, France won.

Who killed the "Princes in the Tower?"

Speaking of Richard III, he is most often pointed to as the perpetrator of this heinous blight on Britain's history.

The princes were Richard's two young nephews—Edward, Prince of Wales and Richard, Duke of York—the first and second heirs to the throne. They were locked in the Tower of London, England's infamous prison, then mysteriously murdered; their bodies were later found under the staircase. Earlier, Richard III's brother, the Duke of Clarence, had also been killed.

The esteemed Shakespeare and Sir Thomas More both agree that Richard III, insecure in his authority and fearing dethronement, called the shots (not being man enough to do it himself). They believe his battlefield defeat at Bosworth Field was fate's justice.

But another investigation builds a more convincing case against Richard's rival, Henry Tudor, who claimed the throne after Richard III's death. If the throne was his ambition all along, then he had a strong motive to kill all the natural heirs—Clarence and the two boys—and use the opportunity to consolidate his Tudor family line (Richard represented the rival house of York). The stuff of TV movies, yes, but let's try to exonerate the unfairly judged whenever possible.

Did Lady Godiva really ride naked through Coventry?

This is not a myth. (Naturally—most of what we were taught in school turns out to be bunko; likewise, preposterous stories like this one turn out to be true.) Her husband in 11th-century England was a strict tax collector, she a real softy. After unsuccessfully appealing to him with logic to lighten the peasants' tax burden, he scoffed that if she was to ride through town unclothed, he'd relent. Presumably, he didn't think she'd take him seriously. She did, he honored his promise, and she remains a heroine of the people to this day. One side note: Before she rode, she asked the townspeople to avert their eyes. All did except for one, a man named Tom. The term "peeping Tom" was thus born!

Where did Chess come from?

Most people think of Chess as a medieval European game, since most of its ornamentations—

especially those of the kings, queens, bishops, and knights—appear that way. In fact, it probably originated in sixth-century India. The Sanskrit name for the game, *Chaturanga,* means "four arms" as well as "army." The four arms are the infantry, cavalry, chariots, and elephants, which correspondingly came to be known in the European game as pawns, knights, bishops, and rooks (or castles). Arab invaders brought the game to Europe around the tenth century, and by the sixteenth century it had taken on its current identity. In Arabic, by the way, it's called *al-schah-mat,* or "the king is dead." Anglicized, this becomes "checkmate."

Why do Americans drive on the right side of the road? Why do the English drive on the left?

Long before there were cars, people tended to keep left. In the Middle Ages, if you saw a guy coming toward you who you didn't know was friend or foe, you'd edge to the left so that your right hand could be poised at your weapon at your side and directed at the stranger (since most people are right-handed, they carried their knives, swords, bayonets, or spiked hammers there). In 1300, the Pope regulated this for all of Europe by insisting that pilgrims on their way to Rome should keep left to avoid traffic jams.

Things changed in America in the late 18th century due to the popularity of Conestoga wagons. these vehicles were drawn by four horses, and the driver rode on the left rear horse so he could whip the animals with his right hand. If he saw another wagon coming, he edged to the right side so he could see that his left wheels didn't touch the opposite wagon's wheels (if he were to edge left, viewing his right wheels would be impossible—this was before side-view mirrors). So we Americans fell into the habit of passing on the right.

Back in England, their wagons were smaller, and being more concerned with appearance than us, they had a seat for the driver. He sat on the right so that when he drew back his whip, it wouldn't get caught on the load behind him, but would instead fly freely through the air. In order to see *his* wheels when passing, he continued to edge left, as was his cultural habit.

Since the automobile was invented, popularized, and mostly manufactured in America, the steering wheel was placed on the left, because that's what we were used to, so driving on the right was further institutionalized. In fact, most other countries found themselves driving on the right as well, because they imported their cars from the U.S.. The exceptions are the ornery British and two of their former colonies, India and Indonesia.

Where did the swastika come from?

It didn't originate with Hitler, that's for sure. Hitler was a grand borrower. He manipulated so many ideas and symbols to fit his own twisted purposes, and did so with such impact, that it's difficult to even imagine a pre-Nazi history to most of them. How can we even think of a swastika again *without* feeling the evil he made it represent?

Yet indeed, its original intentions were decent. Several ancient civilizations used it as a symbol for good fortune (in Sanskrit, swastika means "it is well"), including the Greeks, Mesopotamians, Celts, Chinese, Egyptians, and Native Americans. Even early Christians held it up during the Roman persecution period. Somehow, Hitler believed it represented the purity of "Aryan" breeding, appropriated it, and twisted its arms to point right instead of left.

Who were the Aryans?

"Aryan" is yet another Sanskrit word, meaning "noble." This ancient tribe first appeared near the Caspian Sea, then migrated both east into India and west into Europe around 2000 B.C. Another series of factual errors confused them with the Nordic tribe—Hitler's ideal race of tall, blonde, blue-eyed people.

First, in 1861, a German linguist named Max

Muller attempted to prove that all Indo-European languages were derived from an Aryan tongue. He later admitted he was wrong. But by the 1880s the idea of an Aryan ideal had caught on with the German intelligentsia, who intertwined it with the theories of a French count named Joseph Gobineau. He claimed, in a landmark essay called "The Inequality of Human Races," that the Nordic people were interbreeding out their "naturally strong" racial qualities, mostly by marrying "yellow" and "dark-skinned" people—Gobineau's term was "semitization." The composer Richard Wagner, famed for "Ride of the Valkyries," scored operas that idealized a Nordic paradise. Ironically, Valkyries are descended from Asians. Hitler, too, ignored, altered, and all but obliterated this fact.

When did Persia become Iran?

Okay, so there's a flow here. Iran, you see, means "Land of the Aryans." (Ironically, then, Hitler's Valhalla rightly belongs in Tehran.)

"Persia" comes from Parsa, a region in southern Iran. Somehow, westerners began identifying it as Persia around the sixth century B.C.—that's 25 centuries of misidentification! Iranians have always called it Iran, and in 1935 the government officially requested that everyone else refer to it that way as well (perhaps to help clean up that Hitler mess), although some Iranian immigrants in America refer to themselves as Persian to avoid hostile treatment. Confused?

Did Hitler ever marry Eva Braun?

They tied the knot on the eve of their joint suicide in April, 1945. He met her in the Munich shop of his photographer, where she was a saleswoman, and she soon became his mistress. He never allowed her to appear in public with him, however.

What was the historical significance of the Bubonic Plagues?

Perhaps no other natural event altered the course of history as much as the Bubonic Plague of Justinian, which occurred from 540-590 A.D. and decimated the populations of Europe and Asia. Most people think of the plague as having only occurred in the 14th century, but that was actually the second of three such pandemics.

The Justinian plague was named after the great Byzantine emperor Justinian I, whose legal and architectural innovations are still with us. It struck at the height of his success, carried over from Lower Egypt by traders and scholars. Soon, people were dying at an average of ten thousand a day. Gravediggers stopped trying to keep up: roofs were removed from towers so the buildings could be stacked high with bodies. Armies, cities, and governments were demolished. After fifty years, the death toll was one hundred million people, or about ninety percent of human population in that region of the world.

There were three main historical effects: 1) The fall of the Roman Empire; 2) The institutionalization of Christianity (it was seized upon by the masses as their only hope and comfort); 3) The end of Greek and Roman medicinal practices, which proved utterly useless in the face of the plague.

The only survivors were those who had developed an immunity to it—after a while, the disease had simply run its course of human carriers. Since no one at the time was aware of its cause—flea bites from infected black rats—there was no cure, and the disease returned eight centuries later with a vengeance.

The Black Death, which lasted from 1346 to 1361, killed 27 million people, and is thought of as more devastating because there are more surviving accounts of its horror. It ravished all the major cities of Europe—London, Paris, Madrid, Rome, Amsterdam, and many more. To make matters worse, Pope Clement VI got foolish and desperate in his frustration over the lack of a divine response. He declared 1348 a "Holy Year," and implored the masses of Europe to embark on a pilgrimage to Rome, as if the power in numbers might better impress God. Of course, this caused the disease to run even more rampant. Only ten percent returned home.

Interestingly, many people—Germans especially—began blaming Jews (who were dying as fast as anyone), accusing them of poisoning wells. This ignorant racism would later serve as a point in history to fuel Hitler's fire.

The disease's last major occurrence, the London Plague of 1665-66, lasted only a few months. The bacteria had seemingly weakened, and today is weaker still, although not entirely gone. It's conceivable that a stronger virus could emerge in the future.

How large was the British Empire at its peak?

Too large. After playing on the winning World War I team, the victors got even more spoiled than they already were. Great Britain controlled over 14 million square miles and 450 million people—a quarter of the world's population and land—including India, Pakistan, Ireland, Canada, Australia, Ceylon, and Antiqua, not to mention Scotland and Wales. England itself is about 50,000 square miles around.

Was Mata Hari ever caught?

The most notorious spy of World War I was a Dutch officer's wife named Margaretha

Geertruida Zelle, who changed her name when she became an exotic dancer and then a secret agent. She was arrested in her Paris hotel in February 1917, then shot by firing squad. Some say that, before she was shot, she smiled and winked.

Who was Nobel and why does he have a prize named after him?

Alfred Nobel invented dynamite and several other explosives, becoming rich off the patents. Along the way, he killed his brother and four other men during his experiments with nitroglycerine.

He was a shy man who loved English poetry, and always hoped his inventions would be used to end warfare, not further it. Not one to believe in passing on his wealth to his relatives, he decided in his will in 1895 to establish the Nobel Prizes instead, hoping to better mankind by doing so.

Today, the Nobel Prize is the most prestigious award on the planet, so he must have succeeded. Originally, Nobel created only five awards—for physics, chemistry, medicine, literature, and peace. A category for economics was added in 1968.

The Nobel Foundation is run by six members and a chairman appointed by the Swedish government (Nobel was a Swede), and they oversee the investments. The interest earned determines the amount of the award.

Each prize is voted on by experts in their field, albeit ones exclusively from Sweden; the lone exception is the peace prize, which is decided by a Norwegian committee (it was Nobel's idea of being neighborly, to set an example). Occasionally, biases occur. For some reason, Swedes thumb their noses at American and Russian writers (the first literature prize in 1901 was awarded to a Frenchman, Rene Prudhomme, over Leo Tolstoy; later, Hemingway, Graham Greene, and Vladimir Nabokov were also snubbed in favor of lesser-knowns).

But the Norwegians tend to be bold and dead-on, as in 1935, when they insisted on the controversial choice of anti-Nazi journalist Carl von Ossietsky, who had exposed Hitler's secret rearmament operations. Ossietsky later died in a concentration camp as a result, and when the Nazis invaded Norway, even the judges themselves were arrested.

Sports

Did Abner Doubleday invent baseball?

No. The precursor to baseball, rounders, was brought to America from England. Similar to cricket, rounders is played on a field with four posts that form a square. The object of the game is for a "striker" to hit a ball thrown by a "feeder," then touch all four posts. If he misses the ball three times, hits a foul, gets hit by a thrown ball, or hits a fly which is caught, he is out. Teams switch sides after each player is out.

In the 1830s, a form of rounders was being played by American youth. Then in the '40s, Alexander Cartwright, a New York bank clerk, formed the Knickerbocker Base Ball Club and altered the rules a little to reflect the game as we now know it. In 1849, he took a trip across the country and popularized it all the way to California.

So where did Doubleday come in? Abner was actually a man of great achievement, but not in baseball. He fired the first Union shot at Fort Sumter, was a hero at Gettysburg, became a full colonel, and in 1869 chartered San Francisco's first cable car. But when he was a West Point cadet in 1839, he spent the summer learning the game, since he was unable to get a ride home.

This later became significant just after the turn of the century, when sports equipment manufacturer Albert Spaulding needed to win an argument with a British friend about the origins of what had become America's pastime. He set up a commission to investigate, which turned up one Abner Graves, who had been a schoolboy in Cooperstown, New York in 1839. Graves related a story on hearsay about Doubleday "inventing" the game then and there. The commission loved it, thinking our boy had indeed founded the sport out of thin air. The press, as usual in those days, adopted it as gospel.

Where did the Brooklyn/Los Angeles Dodgers get their name?

In the first half of this century, trolley cars were a common sight in Brooklyn. Between these cars, automobiles, and foot traffic, streets were dense. The most agile pedestrians—those who were able to slip through the crowded streets with swift moves—were called "trolley dodgers." On the field, it obviously helped to be similarly coordinated. Of course, nowadays a more apt name for the L.A. team might be something like "left turn on red light kamikazes."

What's the most unusual sport in American history?

If you think Big Time Wrestling is one of the signs of the apocalypse, try "gouging." Popular in the Ohio River Valley in the early 19th century, the object of this game was to poke out your opponent's eye with your thumbnail. Those who flourished tended to have extra-long thumbnails. What did they win? Ten million dollars per bout? How about an eye patch and an emory board.

Why is a football shaped so strangely?

American football evolved from rugby, which evolved from soccer, which is actually called "football" around the rest of the world, so it's come full circle, in a sense.

Soccer, as we will identify it to lessen confusion, began in the Middle Ages in England. During the eleventh century, the Danes occupied England, arousing such hatred among the British that once the Danes were kicked out, one Englishman dug up a buried soldier's skull and began kicking it around. Others followed. Ouch.

To save their feet, they switched to cow's bladders. Two adjacent towns would kick the inflated bladder around until it reached the center of the other's town. Victory. Eventually, cow bladders were replaced by round balls, and the game was moved to a grass field and officially called "association football." When "association" was shortened to "assoc.," it evolved into the slang "soccer."

In 1823, one frustrated college kid decided to pick up the ball and run with it. This was of course illegal, but then, folks standing around said, "Hey, why not?" The kid's college? Rugby.

Let's move to the colonies, where they were still kicking around soccer balls in Ivy League colleges. In 1874, some boys from Canada's McGill University taught Harvard's soccer players how to play rugby. Harvard's team taught Princeton, Yale, and Columbia, and in the 1880s, rules were altered to change the game from rugby to American football.

Oh yeah, the ball shape. Because rugby required carrying the ball as much as kicking it, it made sense that the ball take on an oblong shape for ease of transport (otherwise, we'd be watching the Fumble Bowl every January). In the American game, players carried the ball even more, so it was tapered further at the ends. In 1906, the forward pass was legalized, and over time, came to dominate play, so still more tapering of the ball was necessary for it to float through the air in such a pretty spiral.

How do certain basketball players seem to hover in the air so long?

It's the shoes. It's got to be the shoes!

No, it's not the shoes, although footwear manufacturers are making a killing by promoting that myth. No, the great basketball hangers—Michael Jordan, Julius Erving, Clyde Drexler, Dominique

Wilkins—have great speed. This allows them to take off on a leap from farther away from the hoop, flattening the arc of their jump. Compared to most players, who seem to jump up and down in one place, they seem to float, all because their momentum carries them a greater horizontal distance than most. Of course, it helps their mystique that, while in mid-air, they switch the ball between hands, twist their bodies, or pass behind their backs, all because they're great athletes.

Note: most of these magical hang-time moments actually last less than one second.

Why does the little town of Green Bay, Wisconsin have a pro football team?

It's a throwback to a bygone era, when teams were mostly fielded by midwestern industrial burgs—the Muncie Flyers, the Racine Legion, the Akron Pros, the Decatur Staleys. Usually, burly guys who worked at the local factory played on the team on the weekends—the stars made as much as $100 a game!

The Indian Packing Company paid for the uniforms for the local Green Bay squad, in exchange for using the name "Packers." All the other teams went out of business or moved to bigger cities, due to the limitations of small town populations supporting the finances of running a team (star salaries, travel, stadium upkeep . . .). The Packers survived, thanks to a group of local businessmen who formed a publicly-owned non-profit organization called the Green Bay Football Corporation. Now, in the era of big-time billion-dollar sports, the antiquated notion that the citizens of a small town can own their own team—and compete both on the field and in the marketplace—is not only charming, it's astonishing.

When did the term "upset" begin being used in a sports context?

Amazingly, most sports experts don't know this one. They still think the greatest surprise victory of all time was the Jets beating the Colts in the third Super Bowl. But check this out.

In the world of horse racing, one horse is considered the greatest of all time, hands down: Man O' War (Secretariat is a close second). Although he never won the Kentucky Derby (by a fluke, he wasn't even entered), he lost only one race in his illustrious career in the 1920s, and always won impressively even though he carried more weight than was considered reasonable. The lone horse who beat him? Upset. Since then, the term has come to refer to any surprise victory by a lesser-regarded competitor.

Will there ever be another .400 hitter?

Will there ever be another Elvis? (Well, okay,

there are *lots* of those). Chances are very slim. Ted Williams hit .406 in 1941, and no one has come close since.

The game is more sophisticated nowadays. Hitters have improved, but so have pitchers—they've added weapons like the slider and the forkball to their arsenal, which also includes the obligatory fastball and curve. Plus, managers have come to rely on relief specialists in the late innings, so there are no more 8th and 9th-inning mop-up "gimme" hits.

Furthermore, the range in talent has narrowed. With the advent of sports as big business, the talent pool has increased so that only the cream of the crop plays in the big leagues, and then only after a few years of serious training. Therefore, the variables have declined. So instead of averages that range from .185 to .400, we see a range from .200 to .360. We've reached the invisible wall of human evolution—the players you watch now may not get any better than this, spitting, scratching and all.

Why do bowling shoes look so ugly?

Now, hold on a minute. In recent years, many young folk think bowling shoes are the coolest, man. Everything is cyclical. At the moment, they're in. Two years from now, they'll be just as ugly as before.

In the early days of kegling, all bowling shoes were black. But then, most bowlers owned their own shoes. With the advent of bowling as amateur recreation, a new fashion cropped up to help please the average Joe and Marge Bowler. Red, green, and orange. Maroon, tan, and aqua. Yikes!

Nowadays, the line bowling shoe manufacturers use is this: their ugliness prevents people from stealing them. (Hey, why not go out and buy a Yugo while you're at it?) Since bowling shoes are rented out at an average of 500 per year, lane owners want to keep the theft rate low. So, what, a big red "11" on the back isn't a dead giveaway?

Why is tennis scored so strangely?

You think love is strange? Well, okay, so it is. Lawn tennis, as exemplified by the Wimbledon Tournament each year, evolved from court tennis, a game popularized by the rotund Henry VIII, which was played indoors and used the ceilings and walls, sort of like racquetball today.

In the Middle Ages, Europeans were preoccupied with the sextant—one-sixth of a circle. Back then, you had to win six sets to end the match, and in so doing you would figuratively complete a circle.

Breaking it down further, since one-sixth of a circle is 60 degrees, and the royalty who played the game decided four points should win a game, each point became worth 15.

Now, if you do the math, it doesn't quite hold up, because you not only needed to win four games of 60 points each (240) to win a set, but you had to win six sets of four as well (6 X 240 = 1440). All told, you've made three full circles to win the match. But, hey, who's counting? Maybe they liked the poetry of that.

But it still doesn't explain why we have to put up with this archaic, illogical system. First of all, no one plays six sets of four anymore—a match now consists of either a best of five sets (in which you must win six games, and by at least two), or a best of three. Furthermore, the 15-30-45-game progression was changed to 15-30-40-game long ago, because the 45 was thought too cumbersome to announce. Confused? Aren't we all.

So why not just revamp the whole thing? Well, Americans have tried and tried. The World Pro Championship League adopted the table tennis system of 21, hoping to attract more fans, since nobody really understands the existing system, and if you're going to pay hard-earned dough to enjoy a sporting event, you should at least know what the score is.

But it didn't work, presumably because tennis originated in England, and the stuffy Wimbledon folks would hear none of it. Tradition, you know. It would be like us revising baseball—and that would be akin to blasphemy.

The Marketplace

Why do Band-Aid bandage wrappers come with that little red string even though no one can ever get it to work?

It's supposed to slit the wrapper as you pull it down. However, in the hands of most people, including this intrepid researcher, that never works—the string just comes easily out of the top, and you end up ripping the paper yourself.

So why doesn't Johnson & Johnson get hip to reality and come up with a new gimmick, one that actually helps? Tradition. When they began the Band-Aid line in the 1920s, the red string was considered a classy touch—it meant you could open the packaging without touching the bandage, thus keeping it sterile.

Then what? Unless you're wearing gloves, in which case you wouldn't need the string, you'd still have to touch the bandage to apply it, right? Of course. We all figured this out long ago. Basically, when there's an open gash spewing blood out of our forehead, we don't care. Just rip the darn thing open. To heck with daintiness.

They've finally gotten our drift. A new line, Flexible Fabric, comes in plastic packaging, with a bit of blue plastic hanging out that says "pull." It works. Wow—and it only took them seventy years to fix it.

What makes Ivory soap float?

Somebody goofed. It's one of those beautiful accident stories—like the discovery of penicillin.

In 1878, entrepreneurs Harley Procter and James Gamble wanted to create a soap that would beat out the other popular white soaps of the day. They did. One year later, a worker overmixed the solution with too much air, causing it to bob to the surface of the bath water. Of course, moms loved this new feature because it meant Junior would play with it in the tub like a submarine (before there were even submarines), thus keeping him in longer and making the act of getting him to take a bath less of a sell job.

Needless to say, Harley and James looked like geniuses, and took all the credit.

What caused the demise of the VW Bug?

It wasn't lack of charisma. The Beetle was not only one of the most popular cars of all time, it still boasts a fanatical following. There are Bug Clubs that throw 30-year birthday parties (for the car, of course), 500,000-mile celebrations, and rallies.

After debuting in America in 1949 when two brothers brought it over from Germany and opened a dealership, the Beetle's sales grew steadily through the '50s, then skyrocketed in the

'60s. It was the perfect counterculture vehicle: the baby boomer population bulge was just coming of driving age, and needed a cheap, reliable starter car; the car's "cuteness" was also cleverly marketed (see: Disney's amiable *Love Bug* films, starring "Herbie"); and it appealed to free-thinking college students (and their professors) who rejected the myth of car-as-fantasy that the big Detroit auto makers were selling them.

It was also revered for its durability. Case in point: Woody Allen's *Sleeper* features a classic scene where the protagonist, having been cryogenically frozen, wakes up several centuries in the future. During a chase scene, he runs into a cave, unearths an old Beetle, gets in, and turns the key. It starts.

But by 1975, times had changed. The boomers grew up, had families, bought bigger cars. The war had ended. The Japanese were selling cheap, reliable, better-handling cars to a new generation. In one year, the bug's sales plummeted from 243,00 to 92,000. The VW folks knew the run was over.

To compete with the Japanese, they launched the Rabbit line, which featured better gas mileage, smoother handling, and more head and leg room than the beloved Beetle. But it wasn't the same.

What is Silly Putty?

It's a mixture of boric acid and silicone oil, among other complex chemical compounds. It was invented in the 1940s by General Electric as a cheap synthetic rubber for use during World War II. One suspects a few bored soldiers were bouncing it, stretching it over their faces, and slapping it on their tattooed arms, because that's what bored kids do with it. After the war, a store owner in New Haven, Connecticut named Paul Hodgson must have realized its potential, because he bought a huge quantity of it, packed it in small eggs, and resold it as Silly Putty.

How does the M&M Company get its M's on its M&M's?

Very carefully. Seriously. A sophisticated printing press stamps the M onto each M (or is it each M&M?). Peanut M&M's, however, are tricky. Sometimes you can find no M on a Peanut M&M, because peanuts come in weird sizes, so some just don't fit into the little M&M slots, thus they remain unsullied by edible ink.

Incidentally, M&M stands for the guys who marketed the candy—Victor Mars and his partner, a "Mr." Merrie.

What is Shell Oil named after?

You might suppose the company has a lot of

offshore oil derricks, and that, after a day's drilling work, somebody was going for a walk on the beach one day and spotted a nifty specimen. Nope.

In the mid-19th century, a London shop owner named Marcus Samuel made a thriving business selling pretty little seashells, so he called his store The Shell Shop. From there, he began importing the shells, and then really made a killing by exporting kerosene through the same channels. Eventually, The Shell Shop became Shell Transport and Trading Company. When the automobile became popular, Samuel was perfectly situated to sell gasoline in the same manner, and the profits were so huge the company was renamed Shell Oil.

Why do *TV Guide* listings begin on Saturday?

After all, those guides that come with the Sunday paper begin, of course, on Sunday. Are the *TV Guide* folks just trying to be different, or even rebellious?

Basically, they were there first, so it's the other way around. When the magazine was first published in 1953, Saturday was a big night for family viewing. "The Jackie Gleason Show," "Your Hit Parade," Your Show of Shows," and "The Original Amateur Hour" were all on that night.

Sunday night was even bigger, but back then there were blue laws in many states that forbade businesses from opening on Sundays, so Sunday sales of *TV Guide* were sparse. The publishers also logically figured they'd cash in on Friday night or Saturday grocery shopping if they started the listings with Saturday. You sure can't argue with success.

Nowadays, there's another good reason for keeping it that way: sports. Quite often, networks won't decide which weekend games they'll show in each region until a few days before the event. So by beginning the week with Saturday, the staff can wait until the absolute last minute before printing the teams' names.

What's the origin of the MGM lion?

A young advertising executive named Howard Dietz, who was employed by the (Samuel) Goldwyn Pictures Corporation, was an alumnus of Columbia University. Columbia's nickname is the Lions, and their football fight song is "Roar, Lion, Roar!" When Goldwyn merged with the Metro Studio and Louis B. Mayer to form MGM, everyone agreed the lion was a classy touch (king of the jungle and all), so it stuck. They named it, what else, Leo.

In 1924, Dietz also coined the phrase "Art for art's sake." Wow, two major contributions to popular culture, and nobody's ever heard of the guy. It's just a good thing he didn't go to college at, say, the University of Minnesota (the Golden Gophers) or UC Santa Cruz (the Sea Slugs).

Are television commercials louder than the programming?

No, it's not just you. The idea behind advertising, as you know, is to get you to notice the ad. Hey! Look at me! *Look at me!!!!* Those sly Madison Avenue devils have figured out a way to further drive their annoying slogans into your brain. It's called *volume compression*.

When the FCC first noticed the problem of commercial blaring, they fixed a level of maximum volume for everything on the tube, programming and commercials. For regular old shows and movies, this is not a problem—there are peaks and valleys in the volume, as you have no doubt noticed. But the advertisers *really* want your attention, so they work around the law by using volume compression, which essentially means that the level of sound in the ad is always at maximum allowable volume. That's why that late-night used car huckster seems to be literally shouting in your face.

Is Avon cosmetics somehow related to Shakespeare (whose hometown was Stratford-upon-Avon)?

Yup. In 1896, a New York City salesman named D.H. McConnell stopped selling books door to door and took up perfume, naming his new venture The California Perfume Company, after that warm, exotic, paradisiacal state on the Pacific coast (hey, it was 1896). It took off, and McConnell soon opened his own scent factory in upstate New York. Fifty years of bellringing later, he changed the name, perhaps not wanting the smell of his perfume to be identified with the lovely aroma of smog.

Being an erudite man who'd always admired The Bard, he renamed his company after Shakespeare's birthplace, thus depriving us of possible bewilderment upon hearing the lilting female-intoned words "California Calling!"

How does a Contac capsule know when to release its "tiny time" pills?

Each of the 900 minuscule pills inside the capsule is the same size, but there are several degrees of digestible waxy coating covering the medicine in each pill. Some have very thin layers of coating, so our digestive system breaks them down almost immediately. Those with thicker layers take 30 minutes, or an hour, or two, or three, right on up to 12 hours, to digest. Once the coating is broken down, the medicine goes to work.

The folks at Contac pride themselves on the efficiency of their product, assuring us that each capsule is designed to dissolve evenly without peaks and valleys.

The concept, by the way, is based on those tiny candy beads that are often used to decorate cakes, just as you suspected.

Potpourri

How does the magic trick work where a woman appears to be sawed in half?

This answer will confirm what you've always suspected: there are two women.

Before the trick begins, there's already a woman—wearing the same costume as the magician's beautiful assistant—hiding underneath the table the box sits on. When the lovely Lulabelle climbs in, the hidden lady climbs up through a trap in the table and assumes the position of the lower half of the girl's body, poking her feet out of the box's holes. She's in a curled position with her head bent forward to her knees. Lulabelle, meanwhile, curls up also, drawing her knees to her chin. Two metal dividers shore up the sides of each "half" of the box, and nothing but air is in the middle when the great Blowhardini saws between the two.

Amazingly, this stunt has been a staple on the magic circuit since 1921, and yet it never fails to draw gasps of awe from otherwise rational spectators to this day.

Why are stoplights red, yellow, and green?

It goes back to the railroads. When the tracks began in the 1830s, they needed a safety system.

Red was obvious for "stop." It's the color of blood, and it was used in danger signs for thousands of years. But the railroads didn't care about the others, haphazardly choosing green for "caution" and white for "go."

But problems ensued. Some conductors confused the white light of street lamps for the "go" signal, and on one particular occasion, the red filter fell out of its holder, exposing a white light that was interpreted as "go," and thus causing a horrible crash.

After that, they changed the system to the one we use today. The important thing was to eliminate white, so they arbitrarily chose green for go, yellow for caution, and kept red for stop. A white light would mean one of the three had malfunctioned, and the conductor would know to stop his train. It worked so well that city engineers adopted it for automobile traffic, beginning in Cleveland in 1914.

And by the way, according to law, yellow still means caution, and not "floor it."

What is the line of presidential succession if both the newly-elected president and vice-president were to die between November and the January inauguration?

This is tricky. After the inauguration, it's spelled out: next in line is the Speaker of the House. But before the inauguration, it's dependent on whether the electoral college has met yet.

You've heard of electoral votes—when you watch election results, you see the popular tally and the electoral tally. In our system, when we vote for president, we actually vote for electoral representatives, who are obliged to cast their votes accordingly in the electoral college, which meets several weeks after the popular election. A fussy middle step perhaps, but it's been there from day one.

So if the Prez-elect and Veep-elect die before the electoral college meets, it's up to the college to decide. Presumably, the winning party's electors would choose new candidates and vote them in. But they don't have to.

If the President and his mate succumb *after* the meeting, we're in trouble. There is no law for this. Would chaos and anarchy result? Nah. Congress would just call an emergency meeting and brainstorm something. Then again, maybe that *would* be chaotic. Keep this in mind the next time you choose a congressperson.

How are television ratings measured and processed so quickly?

Hey, it's the '90s. We got faxes, we got computers, we got instant TV ratings.

The A.C. Nielsen Company was founded in 1923 to survey usage of industrial machinery. By

1950, being visionaries of sorts, they had moved into communications, setting themselves up with a virtual monopoly on TV ratings ever since. Their data is so important in the television business that a minor point fluctuation can make or break a program, and the combined results of each station and network determines their advertising rates. Points equal dollars, but you knew that.

The amazing thing is that the survey is so small. Only 1,200 homes are "Nielsen families," but they are selected carefully to represent the entire population. They choose homes geographically, based on U.S. Census figures, then later ask each household member to fill out a detailed form.

The form is for specifics like age, sex, race, income, and education, that sort of thing. But the real deal is a device that records all television usage in the house—when it's on, when it's off, all channel switchings, all tube doings—and feeds the info by phone into a main computer at Nielsen headquarters. The computer processes the results of each home each day, so by Wednesday morning we can read in the paper how many of us watched Monday Night Football.

Why is a mile 5,280 feet? Why not 5,000 feet?

Don't blame the Romans. For them, a mile *was* 5,000 feet. They measured in paces—two steps to the pace, each pace about five feet, so a thousand paces, or *milia passum,* measured roughly 5,000 feet.

The British adopted this system, but made one adjustment. For them, the furlong—660 feet—was the basic unit of long measurement, because it was the length of a plowed furrow in a farmer's field. They figured it would be jolly good if a mile could be divided into an even number of furlongs. Since eight furlongs equals 5,280 feet, Parliament suggested to Queen Elizabeth I in 1575 to officially add the extra 280. And so she did.

Why do we dress our baby boys in blue and our baby girls in pink?

Long, long ago, when infant mortality rates were quite high (you could have ten babies and perhaps two of them survived), it was vitally important to protect baby boys as much as possible, since they were considered the breadwinners/hunters/heads of future families. In those days, it was thought that evil spirits were plaguing babies, so our ancestors chose to swathe the male tots in blue, because blue is the color of the heavens, and the heavens would thus defend the little guy against the satanic forces. (Even today, many Arabs paint their doorways blue for the same reason.) Little girls, however, were not considered as important, so they neglected to give them a color. Only in the last century did parents catch on to the fact that the girls were feeling left out, so for them the dainty pink was the obvious choice.

When we address a letter, why do we need to bother with the city and state, if those are defined by the zip code?

Your correspondent even has an out-of-town friend who insists on proving this fact by including only a name and a zip code on the envelope.

Indeed, the post office will deliver mail addressed by these cranks, but it's none too happy about it. Cities and states, you see, serve a valuable purpose as a cross-check, since many people inadvertently transpose digits in zip codes, or write them illegibly. Nines look like fours, threes look like eights, that sort of thing. If any of this is wrong, back it goes to the sender.

Also, in some rural areas, neighboring communities share the same zip code, so the poor mailman won't know exactly which little burg you live in. So by going that extra mile, you'll help your letter go that extra day or two faster.

What is a radial tire, and how does it grip a wet road?

A radial tire has rope-like cords inside of it, each at a 90-degree angle to the road, sort of like a bicycle's spokes. It makes the tire more efficient in its grip of the road, and therefore longer-lasting. Most radials are also steel-belted, which actually means that two or four belts made of steel wrap around the tire, but underneath the tread, to help stabilize it and protect it from glass and other potentially damaging road hazards.

If roads were always dry, the most efficient tire would be a very wide, smooth one that is in constant contact with the road, like those big fat ones on dragsters. But since precipitation is a fact of life, our tires need fancy tread designs to channel water away from the tire. Without those treads, your car would hydroplane—this actually means you car floats like a boat—on wet roads, because there is no friction. No friction, no control, no safety. So the treads are cut in a zig-zag-like design across the tire, because this type of pattern has been found to be the most efficient at shooting water out to each side.

How are underwater tunnels constructed?

Amazingly, underwater tunnels have been built since the mid-19th century. In those days, it was more problematic, of course. They just started digging, first vertically down into the ground on land deep enough to get under the water, then horizontally in the direction of the tunnel. As they dug, they pumped air in to hold up the walls so that the air pressure inside was greater than the water pressure outside, thus preventing the walls from collapsing. They would then shore up the inside walls with cement, and pump out any leaking water.

In this century, the more efficient method is to build the segments on dry land first, then lower them into the water. But before lowering, a trench is dug with underwater tools, then pillars are pushed even deeper into the ground to hold the big tube so that it sits at the same level throughout its length. When this foundation is ready, the pieces are dropped in (each with air-tight gates on its ends so that water doesn't fill it), and the segments are joined by workers inside.

Why do newspapers and magazines always force you to continue reading an article in the back pages, instead of confining it to one area?

Some editors are just now getting hip to how truly annoying this is to most people, but few major magazines and virtually no newspapers have changed their policies about this (some intrepid newer, younger-oriented magazines use their lack of continuation as a selling point).

It's not likely that newspapers will ever change on this point, because their front page is what sells the paper. If there were only one story on the front page, it would only appeal to a select few. What's more, the front page has come to symbolize all the important news, so that someone just glancing at it can scan the headlines and know essentially what's going on in the world.

But magazines are more flexible, to a degree. Their reasons for continuation are twofold. First, they'll sell advertising space to virtually anyone, in virtually any size or configuration. If they can't fill the rest of a page with complementary ads, it becomes necessary to fill it with spare editorial content—namely, the back section of an article. Second, in the magazine world, it's important to give readers an impression that editorial content is their sole reason for existing, and to that end, all magazines tend to put their front-line feature articles in a block of pages in the middle, with little or no advertising separating them. Confining several beginnings to this small-ish space necessitates rerouting their endings further back.

Moreover, there are costs to consider. Most of the middle-section articles tend to be laid out with eye-catching color graphics, but most magazines can't afford to make every page in color, so they prioritize by putting the front halves of the lead stories on the allotted color pages and continuing them on black-and-white pages in the back.

Since the publishing business is so competitive, it would seem natural that more aggressive magazines would opt for total non-continuation, and some do. As long as they can afford to do so.

How do dollar-bill changers know if your dollar is authentic? How does it know the difference between a single and a five, or ten, or twenty?

Been trying to cheat it with Monopoly money? Xeroxes? Paper pesos? No dice, pal.

There are five authenticity tests in a bill changer. The first one is a light that measures the bill's thickness as it's entering—that's why it won't take newsprint or some other impostor. Once the bill's in, another light source checks for very fine lines in the words "one dollar," or in other cases, "five dollars," or what have you. A third test scans it for magnetic characteristics in the ink with which the U.S. mint prints. The fourth test is actually a double-check that verifies the first three. Finally, the bill is measured for correct length.

After all five tests are passed, you get your quarters.